The social history of Canada

MICHAEL BLISS, EDITOR

OR THE RELIGION OF THE NEW AGE

The new Christianity

SALEM GOLDWORTH BLAND

INTRODUCTION BY RICHARD ALLEN

UNIVERSITY OF TORONTO PRESS

© University of Toronto Press 1973

Toronto and Buffalo

Printed in Canada

ISBN (casebound) 0-8020-1954-4

ISBN (paperback) 0-8020-6179-6

Microfiche ISBN 0-8020-0298-6

LC 72-95815

The original edition of this work appeared in 1920

An introduction

RICHARD ALLEN

'In a very short time it will be acclaimed from every revolutionary platform; and ... it will lend to the revolutionary movement an air of religious sanction ...'[1] It was mid-June 1920. Lieutenant-Colonel C.F. Hamilton, the intelligence and liaison officer of the Royal Canadian Mounted Police, had just read the recently published *New Christianity* by Salem Bland, the stormy petrel of Canadian Protestantism. He sized it up quickly, and dashed a letter off to T. Albert Moore, head of the Methodist Department of Evangelism and Social Service, in an attempt to enlist Moore's aid in undermining the public reception of the book.

Hamilton was not alarmed without reason. Unrest was pulsing through the entire western world, and Canada had been in an unsteady state since the late war years. The conscription crisis had triggered a new wave of both agrarian and labour radicalism. Returning soldiers were in a volatile mood, occasionally storming factories to demand jobs. Wartime propaganda had utilized the prewar language of social reform, and many were calling for the redemption of those rhetorical promises, not least of all the churches. In 1918 the Methodist Church had called for a 'complete social reconstruction' transferring the basis of the economy from competition and profits to co-operation and service. On the other hand, those who saw wartime mobilization of private industry as a temporary measure only justifiable in a time of national peril had organized their forces in a National Reconstruction Association to hasten a return to prewar conditions of relative governmental non-interference. The clash of forces had come in the strikes of mid-1919, the greatest of which had been the Winnipeg general sympathetic strike of May and June. The industrial unionism of the One Big Union had since then split the ranks of labour, but if the cry for direct action had begun to wane a little, labour political militancy was on the rise, and labour churches, devoted to a mixture of Christian, labour, and socialist ideals, were spreading across the nation. The great farm organizations were girding themselves for political action, and already, with labour, had taken over the provincial administration of Ontario. To some it seemed that class politics was about to replace the traditional party system. Hamilton could well agree with the powerful metaphor beginning Bland's book, that the western nations were 'like storm-tossed sailors who, after a desperate voyage, have reached land only to find it heaving with earthquakes.'

Salem Bland was not a young radical, but a seasoned Methodist clergyman, recently a professor at Wesley College, Winnipeg, and now pastor of Broadway Methodist Tabernacle in Toronto. Since his earliest ministry in the St Lawrence and Ottawa valleys, he had been pressing his church forward onto new frontiers. *The New Christianity* was entirely in character. In it Bland attempted to place the unrest of the times in a large historical perspective and brought social, political, and economic developments into conjunction with the main trends of religion in recent decades. His central theme was that the processes of industrial and social consolidation, the growth of organized labour, and the spread of sociological ideas, especially in the church, spelled the end of the old order of capitalism and Protestantism which had dominated most of western Christendom for three centuries. In support of this position he described the progressive march of democracy from the twelfth- and thirteenth-century universities, into religion in the Protestant Reformation of the sixteenth century, into politics in the nineteenth century, and now unmistakably making its way in the world of industry. Allied to democracy was the spirit of brotherhood, planted by Christ in his church, compromised by a 'perverse exaltation of dogma and orthodoxy' over the centuries, but now being rediscovered by movements both inside and outside the church and becoming 'the master passion' of the day.

The primary impediment to the full realization of democracy and brotherhood, Bland argued, was modern capitalism based on private property rights in industry and motivated by a competitive individualism. The distinctive task of the age, then, was the abolition of capitalism. For Bland that was as much a religious as a secular objective, for, in keeping with the Social Gospel he had espoused for over a generation, salvation was not a matter of heavenly reward but the restoration of right relations among men on earth. Industrial combinations, co-operatives, trade unions, public ownership, insurance schemes, industrial councils, and so on, all taught men to think socially; and therefore to attack and discredit them was to oppose what Christianity was all about.

The second impediment to a new social order embodying the Christian spirit, however, was the almost absolute attachment of Christians to their respective traditions. None of the prevailing churches was in entire harmony with the needs of the new age,

Protestantism least of all. To provide a basis for Christian advance, Bland therefore drew upon recent historical analysis of the changing relationships of Christianity and culture. Devotion to Jesus Christ was the essential kernel of Christianity, he suggested, but the dogmatic and institutional forms of its expression were 'subject to the same influences as fashion the changing social order.' The chief of those influences were economics and race.

In western civilization, Bland thought, Christianity had gone through two phases of interaction with the economic order and was now entering a third. The insecurity of life in the feudal period had led to emphases on institutional order and otherworldliness which marked Roman Catholicism. The expansion of every aspect of life, but primarily the economic, in the fifteenth through the seventeenth centuries brought a new spirit into church life reflecting 'freedom-loving, self-reliant, ambitious burghers.' They infused into the new Protestant movement a primary concern with the economic virtues of industry, thrift, sobriety, honesty, and self-control, and with the uneconomic vices of indolence, intemperance, licentiousness, and poverty. Humility and compassion fell to a low ebb, and preoccupation with individual character became pronounced.

The new power of labour, Bland suggested, marked the end of bourgeois Christianity and the inception of a labour Christianity dominated by the values of labour, namely the virtue of solidarity, and the duty and right of all to productive labour, to a living wage, and to union or association. To fulfil its destiny the labour movement would have to broaden itself to include all creative work and recognize its Christian and religious character. To so interpret labour to itself was the prophetic task of the hour. It was equally important to convince the churches of that. Bland was more than a little anxious about Protestantism in this regard, for except in isolated and unofficial cases Protestant ideology had given little sanction to the struggles of labour. He therefore reserved his strongest criticism for his own Protestant tradition, while he saw a more direct relevance to the new social age in the corporate spirit of Catholicism.

Bland knew as well as anyone that the phrase 'bourgeois Christianity' did not express the sum of Protestantism (though he feared it might be its nemesis), and that 'labour Christianity' would have to be more than a gloss on an economic movement. He therefore went on to discuss what he loosely called the 'racial impact' on Christianity, although by that he meant something less biological than cultural. Jews, Greeks, Latins, Teutons, all had evolved peculiar forms of Christian life. Another form was being added in North America. With the Jewish it would be simple in creed, emphasizing the ethical, but would take a progressive rather than an apocalyptic view of history. With the Greek it would be inquisitive and speculative, but would reject later Greek orthodoxy. With the Latin it would show a genius for organization and a catholicity of peoples, but would reject a priestly hierarchy for lay leadership and democracy. With the Teutonic it would be free and unceremonious, and stress personal dignity without succumbing to individualism. American Christianity would be a social religion which would keep the figure of Jesus Christ primary, even when it did not recognize his divinity.

The chief hope of the future lay in a marriage of Bland's labour Christianity and American Christianity. However, the age was also one of international consolidation, and overarching all of Bland's particular hopes was that of a 'Great Christianity' which would accommodate all the older traditions along with those that were emerging in the new world and out of the African and Oriental missions — a glimmering of the worldwide ecumenical movement of our own time. He was an ardent enough nationalist to hope that the church union movement in Canada would lead the way in breaking out from the traditional structures of Protestant church life. In that he was not wrong, but whether it has been the pathfinder for the substance of his New Christianity is another matter.

The book clearly was not a piece of academic history or theology. Indeed, it could be called Salem Bland's longest sermon, and had many of the weaknesses of that genre when reduced to print. Nevertheless, it presented a powerful strategic standpoint. It provided Canadian Christians — that is, most Canadians — with the resources necessary for liberation from the tyranny of their traditions. It offered Canadian labour and radical reform all the bulwarks of essential Christianity. At the same time that it gave some sanction to the labour churches, it established perspectives and endorsed objectives which would make those churches unnecessary. Its theoretical dissociation of the essence of Christianity from its cultural expression offered a counterpoise to both the fact and the charges of church domination by the middle and wealthy classes. If it treated Protestantism more harshly than Roman Catholicism, to have softened its criticism would have drawn the stinger for Protestants from the historical scandal Bland was addressing.

The central ideas of *The New Christianity* are no novelty to the later twentieth century, but in 1920 they were still controversial even in the academic world. There had been considerable discussion of the congruence of capitalism and Protestantism, especially by Catholics and Marxists attacking Protestantism and religion respectively. To many orthodox Protestants, the espousing of such positions by a Protestant clergyman must have seemed arch-apostasy. To many Protestant social reformers it would be a matter of concern to think that, having exposed themselves to criticism by questioning the capitalist order, they could not consistently seek refuge in traditional Protestant sanctuaries.

Certain of Bland's categories would not be new to informed readers. The idea of a dialectical unity of culture and religion which underlay the book was a product of what has been called the 'uniformitarian' cast of mind evolved in the previous century. In various ways Herder, Hegel, Marx, Comte, de Gobineau, Sombart, and Spengler had applied the concept that the collectivities of nation, race, and civilization might have unified 'lives' of their own, and Burckhardt had given it classical historical expression in his history of the renaissance in Italy. That Christianity absorbed much from its cultural setting was a commonplace with George Munro Grant of Queen's University in the 1890s. Bland's characterization of Jewish, Greek, Roman, and Teutonic (Anglo-Saxon) civilization was a long-standing idea used by Josiah Strong in his widely read *The New Era* (1893), an early American social gospel work. That American conditions had bred a democratic spirit in North American Christianity was widely commented on in Methodist circles after W.J. Dawson's lectures to the Methodist Ecumenical Congress in New York in 1891. And Walter Rauschenbusch, the dean of American social gospellers, popularized the idea that labour and Christianity would come into their kingdom together or not at all in his *Christianity and the Social Crisis* (1907). Nor was the title of Bland's work original. Saint Simon, the eccentric grandfather of positivism and sociology, had written a piece under the title of *The New Christianity* a century before, and it is intriguing that Bland's first use of the phrase in 1896 roughly coincided with his first equivocal encounter with the work of Saint Simon's disciple, Auguste Comte.[2]

While Bland's book was not offered with any pretence of originality, it is worth noting that neither Bland nor most of his readers had the benefit of the sophisticated historical analysis of the church's dogma, social teaching, and ethos associated with Harnack, Troeltsch, and Weber. Their great turn of the century works remained largely untranslated in 1920. Tawney's celebrated lectures were not given until 1922, and not published as *Religion and the Rise of Capitalism* until 1926; and Richard Niebuhr's classic, *The Social Sources of Denominationalism,* was not in print until 1929. Furthermore, in evaluating Bland's originality, it must be borne in mind that the perspectives of *The New Christianity* were largely in his mind in the 1890s and derived from many sources. However, Bland was not writing a treatise for the few but a tract for the many. He was playing the role to which he had called his fellow pastors in 1895, to be popularizers of the new and fruitful ideas of the age. No one could reasonably deny that, whatever the background of the ideas in it, his book was a potent instrument in the context of postwar unrest in Canada.

The New Christianity was one of several books appearing after the war, surveying the Canadian scene and urging various reforms. C.W. Peterson's *Wake Up Canada!*, J.O. Miller's *The New Era in Canada,* William Irvine's *Farmers in Politics* (to which Bland contributed the foreword), and W.L. Mackenzie King's *Industry and Humanity,* were the chief of these. Bland's work was the most radical in its proposals and implications. With King's book it shares the distinction of being one of that rare breed of attempts to survey Canadian developments in terms of large principles of analysis or historical development. Lieutenant-Colonel Hamilton understood this fact when he wrote Moore that 'in this country as a rule there is little discussion of principles.' He was therefore concerned that the book would 'be given a few eulogistic reviews' and then dropped, and asked if it would not be advisable 'to subject to a reasonably energetic examination a book which declares that Protestantism "will not survive," and ignores its work in promoting humanitarian endeavour, and which declares that to criticize public ownership is to commit the sin against the Holy Ghost?'

Moore did his work – a lengthy review in the *Christian Guardian* declared that the book was 'not a logical and reasoned advocacy of the rights of Labor; the author apparently aims [rather] to challenge the attention than to convince ... Few of his readers, probably, will agree with all the author's statements, and probably he does not expect them to ...'[3] Bland noted with disappointment: 'not a good word for it. Compare the other reviews.' Three months later, however, Ernest Thomas, one of the most able minds in the church, more than redressed the balance in an article in the *Guardian* declaring the book to be an incisive presentation of main currents and indisputable facts.[4]

The book could not fail to be controversial. Father L. Minehan of Toronto thought that its small amount of wisdom had already been given to the world by Leo XIII and the pastoral letter of Catholic bishops of the United States in 1919.[5] The Baptist arch-fundamentalist, the Reverend T.T. Shields, thought the book should be very useful to many because 'the truth is generally to be found in the opposite of what he [Bland] says.'[6] The editor of the *Presbyterian and Westminster,* while disagreeing with much, felt it a very valuable contribution to the debate on social questions.[7] The Reverend A.E. Ribourg of St Alban's Cathedral (Anglican), however, was in considerable agreement with many of Bland's arguments.[8] Methodist reactions were as diverse as all of these.[9]

The *Toronto Daily Star* on June 1 treated the book as front-page news, but it was in the west that the book was most enthusiastically received. Professor W.T. Allison, writing in the *Edmonton Journal,* thought that parts of the book were brilliant.[10] The *Grain Growers' Guide* concurred and sold the book through its book department.[11] The *Saskatoon Daily Star,* noting that *The New Christianity* was being widely read, reflected that 'one reads the book with the feeling that this is just what he has thought all his life, but lacked the power of expression to put it into words ... [It] is a concentrated form of the message which ministers are sending forth from pulpits today.'[12]

The book's only adverse reception in the west came from the Bookman in the *Manitoba Free Press.* The *Free Press* had bitterly opposed the general strike; its reviewer thought Bland had entirely misread the character of labour, whose 'cruel processes' would hardly further the Christian ethic.[13]

Bland had a warm relationship with a number of labour leaders, like Fred Tipping of the Winnipeg Trades and Labour Council and James Simpson, a vice-president of the Trades and Labour Congress, a leading figure in the Ontario Independent Labor Party, and editor

of the *Industrial Banner*. Simpson spoke for such men when he
hoped that workers would take the broad concepts of *The New
Christianity* to heart and learn to think in such high terms of their
mission.[14] For some time the notion that Jesus and the earliest
church were the first socialists had played a role in legitimizing
socialism,[15] and it was part of the creed of Marxists like Dr W.J.
Curry, a Chilliwack dentist and member of the Socialist Party of
Canada in British Columbia, that the religious life of the nation
would shift with its economic base.[16] It is difficult to doubt that the
book found its way onto the very platforms the RCMP feared.

Bland considered that it had taken some courage for the publish-
er, McClelland and Stewart, to issue the book in the first place, but
when within a year *The New Christianity* was sold out, suggestions
of a second edition were not taken up.[17] Had the hand of the RCMP
reached beyond the church to the press as well?

Fifty years later, the reprinting of the book is important, not
because it was an irritant to the RCMP, nor just because it represents
an instance of the Social Gospel interpreting the postwar crisis in
Canada. It is not an especially good indication of the breadth and
depth of the mind of its author. Its chief significance lies rather in its
intellectual lineage, which is an instructive study in how the highest
traditions of evangelical Christianity came into radical conjunction
with the currents of economic change, social reform, and political
upheaval in Canada in the first decades of this century.

The background of *The New Christianity* begins with Salem's
father, Henry Flesher Bland, who had been a minor but expanding Yorkshire woollens manufacturer of mid-nineteenth-century
England and was devoted to the twin gospels of education and
Methodism. He expected the two 'god-like elements of knowledge
and love' not only to prepare men for heaven where all distinctions
and all the fictitious lines of demarcation on earth would disappear,
but also to revolutionize everything absurd in the customs of
society.[18] When his business jeopardized his lay preaching he sold his
mills and came to Canada in 1858 to become one of the foremost
ministers of the Methodist Church. His belief that children were
born in a state of grace stood in sharp contrast to the prevailing
views of most churchmen that children were born in original sin; his
outspoken preaching, writing, and innovation in church practice on
the subject did much to inject a hopeful view of childhood into the

Canadian mind, providing, thereby, an indispensable foundation for the later work of social reform.[19]

Salem Bland, beginning his ministry in 1880, appropriated these views and soon pressed beyond them. Like his father he was very much a child of the age of improvement, but he was even more prone to see spiritual and moral significance in the material progress of the age, to preach that personal perfection was possible in this life, and to anticipate a millennial climax to history itself.[20] Already in the early 1880s he was protesting against the doctrine of the dualism of body and soul and asserting that salvation pertained to the whole being, to the restoration of man to a fullness of bodily, mental, and spiritual health. He resolved not to preach about heaven but to challenge his hearers to be a genuine people of change, ready to go with Christ 'even into exile from heaven, to realize a heaven here.'[21] Given the prevalence of the evangelical mind in late nineteenth- and early twentieth-century Canada, it is difficult to make too much of the critical relocation of salvation in this transition from the elder to the younger Bland. Implied in the latter's early thought was not only the notion of the body as a living temple, which informed so much of the prohibition, personal purity, and public health movements, but also a thorough – even revolutionary – concept of the need for change in the quality of social life as a whole.

In the early 1880s Bland's ideal Christian was still the evangelical version of aggressive Protestant individualism. He himself was active in sabbath and temperance reform. While both reforms could be used to buttress a disciplined commercial ethic, Bland was more prone to use them to flay the idolatry of business values and the rapacity of industrial practices.[22] At mid-decade, however, ten years of profound development began. The writings of Charles Kingsley and Thoreau deepened his appreciation of nature. Principal Grant of Queen's University encouraged him to speak out on subjects of practical morality and to reconsider his harsh views of Roman Catholicism. Kingsley again, with Robert Browning, Matthew Arnold, George Eliot, and others, helped him to resolve a lingering conflict over the claims of culture and religion. Religion, he came to believe, concerned not simply an interior transaction between the soul and God, but the awakening of a larger self turned outward to the needs and thoughts of others – and hence embracing the entire range of culture – a position which brought him into direct conflict with the church's restrictive code of discipline.

No sooner was Bland reaching such conclusions than his reading of Ruskin, Henry George, and Tolstoy, as well as the literature of emerging social Christianity in Britain and the United States, broadened the whole social basis of his outlook. His Methodism had never permitted him to adopt the social Darwinism of Spencer and Sumner, but Henry Drummond, Kropotkin, and Benjamin Kidd convinced him of what he already suspected, that the devices and ends of evolution were the social graces rather than competition. It was finally with the aid of Hegelianism in the mid-nineties that he was able to synthesize his new ideas with a grand concept of the movement and nature of both history and Christianity.[23]

The ideas Bland was wrestling with and bringing to a satisfying resolution were, however, making havoc of the traditional views of many Christians both in pulpit and pew. In the Christian view the meaning of nature, man, and history was given by God. For many that revelation was seen as conveyed in a restricted, often literal and mechanical way, by one man, Jesus; one book, the Bible; one agency, the Church. Such static conceptions could hardly accommodate the dynamic post-Darwinian world-view. For Bland, however, the new outlook fertilized biblical conceptions. St Paul was peculiarly amenable to reinterpretation and yielded a harvest of new insights. The English philosopher, Edward Caird, persuaded Bland of the validity of a progressive revelation. The historical critics of scripture reconstructed the foundation works of the Old Testament and showed how the great prophetic tradition stood at the peak of Hebraic religion, and had been the product of long development. The prophets were not simply predictors of a coming Messiah, but giants of ethical insight who could read the signs of the times and fearlessly propound their political implications. Surely, then, they were the model for those of every age who sensed that God had not locked His word to mankind into one book or people or historical age. However normative scripture might be, or however representative the history of the Jewish people, revelation (God's will for man) had to be sought anew amid the struggles of one's own time.

Others were reaching towards similar conclusions, but in the forum where Bland tried out his ripest conclusions in the 1890s, the Queen's Alumni Conferences, he was invariably the most open in his approach to new thought, the most comprehensive in his interests, and the most radical in his applications.[24] In an 1896 sermon on the all-encompassing liberty of the Christian man he first used the term the 'new Christianity.'[25] Three years later, before a large convention of Ontario young people, he took the phrase as the title of his address. The 'old Christianity' had often sung that 'this world's a wilderness of woe,' but that was to let the 'hope of heaven ... corrupt us, divert us from concern for [the] miserable and oppressed ...' The 'new Christianity' would set aside that strain of escapism and adopt 'the idea of conquest.' It would not take its Pilgrim out of the City of Destruction, but leave him there 'amid its sins and miseries, starting a College settlement, a mission church, or a Salvation Army Barracks, a Good Government Club or a Municipal Reform Association, resolute to transform the City of Destruction into a City of Salvation.' Christians, he concluded, 'cannot permanently acquiesce in a society organized on unchristian principles.'[26] Bland's address to the young people marked his transformation of the older evangelicalism into an explicitly social faith.

Part of the confidence with which Bland announced the new Christianity of 1899 derived from the expansion of evangelical Christianity in North America throughout the nineteenth century. By 1891 his own church, the Methodist Church in Canada, had become the largest Protestant denomination in the nation, its spirit broadening as it took up an ever more comprehensive culture-building role.[27] The currents of progressivism were finding their way into the church and, in 1896, in the first of a notable series of social declarations, it pitted the teachings of Jesus against the 'heartless combinations' of the age.[28]

By the time Bland left the east for Wesley College, Winnipeg, in 1903, he had become an outspoken advocate of extensive state provision of cultural amenities and social schemes to equalize conditions in society. He was a single taxer, a convinced democrat, and a defender of labour's rights to organize. He took a hopeful view of the large trend to business combination, believing it would nurture a more social spirit, possibly even among the owners and managers of industry, but he urged the devices of co-operation and public ownership as most congruent to the trend itself and to the ends he had in mind. He had no ties with the agrarian reform movement of Ontario in the 1890s, although he had manifested some sympathy with the

American populists of the decade. He had grown up and worked chiefly in the middle-sized industrial and commercial centres of Ontario – Dundas, Kingston, Cornwall, Smith's Falls, Ottawa – most of them cities whose future was very much in question in that decade of transition to large-scale industry.[29] While he saw clearly the profound illness of the great cities, he did not react negatively to them, but believed that mankind would find its highest fulfilment in the city.[30] He had also lived for a number of years in Quebec and Montreal and by the 1890s had developed his sympathies with Roman Catholicism to the point where he opposed the overwhelming majority of his colleagues on the Jesuit Estates and Manitoba schools crises.[31] He had become a proponent of Protestant church union, and already was giving voice to ideas that would bring all Christian traditions together regardless of temperament, structure, or doctrine. Heresy did not consist in error, he said, for error was necessary to truth. Heresy was to be possessed of a spirit of faction,[32] an interpretation obviously germane to the social role to which he was calling the church.

Twenty years before the publication of *The New Christianity*, then, Bland had reached all the essential positions expressed in it. He was not, as has been thought, a western radical, but an eastern radical who moved west and readily took up its causes, a pattern frequent enough in the western radical tradition to suggest the need for a more careful examination of its origin and character. In sixteen years, Bland's role in the west was that of a teacher and popularizer of the new currents of biblical studies, of liberal theology, and of Christian social thought and action. His students, William Irvine, who was instrumental in bringing the United Farmers of Alberta into politics, and William Ivens, who founded the labour churches in the west, were only two of many who were so influenced by Bland that they could not keep themselves or their religion out of the progressive endeavours of the time. Bland himself was a revered figure in the prohibition, single tax, and direct legislation movements, an advocate of free trade, and a member of that shining constellation of Winnipeg reformers that included Fred Tipping, a president of the Trades and Labour Council; F.J. Dixon, the single taxer; S.J. Farmer of the Direct Legislation League; A.W. Puttee, editor of the labour paper, the *Voice;* George F. Chipman, editor of the *Grain Growers' Guide;* A.V. Thomas, editorial writer for the *Winnipeg Tribune;*

J.S. Woodsworth of All Peoples' Mission; C.W. Gordon, Presbyterian minister, author (Ralph Connor), prohibition leader, and industrial conciliator; and D.S. Hamilton, the Congregationalist minister who became the first judge of the Manitoba Juvenile Court.

Throughout his sixteen years in the west Bland was in constant demand both as a preacher and public speaker, and came to be regarded by many as one of the most powerful preachers and platform orators in the country. He had great expectations of the co-operative organizations the grain growers were spawning, and by 1913 was convinced they should enter politics as the core of a new party, even sparking an abortive revolt in that direction at the Saskatchewan Grain Growers' Convention of 1913. Not surprisingly, there had been attempts to rein in so outspoken a figure as early as 1907, and when he was dismissed from Wesley College in 1917 in controversial circumstances, there was a considerable storm throughout the west.[33]

It was symbolic of his position at the end of his period in the west that in the fall and winter of 1918-19 he attended the National Convention of the Trades and Labour Congress in Quebec to gauge the strength of radical forces there; the General Conference of his church in Hamilton, where he was the *éminence grise* behind its advanced social manifesto; and the Saskatchewan Grain Growers' Convention in Regina, where he gave the keynote address, once more calling the farmers to political action. For years some believed he was one of the architects of the Winnipeg general sympathetic strike of mid-1919, but he had left the west even before the critical Western Labor Conference of March.

It would be easy to press Bland too far to the forefront of the Social Gospel in Canada, chiefly because he lived so long and associated himself with so many movements of social reform. By 1920, however, there had been a small host of outstanding men and women motivated by the social passion. There had been S.S. Craig, the Presbyterian minister who had campaigned for Henry George, the great proponent of land reform and the single tax, in the mayoralty contest in New York in 1886, and later established an independent social reform pulpit in Toronto. There was Elliott S. Rowe, the Toronto Methodist minister who was president of the Social Progress Company which published the socialist paper, *Citizen and Country*, with George Wrigley, an Anglican and head of the Direct

Legislation League in Canada, as its editor. There was F.S. Spence, a
Methodist and a Toronto alderman, who was a tireless campaigner
for prohibition, public ownership, and the rights of labour. S.D.
Chown, Methodist, in 1902 became the head of the first church
department anywhere to devote itself to the causes of the Social
Gospel. J.G. Shearer did the same in the Presbyterian Church after
creating the church-labour alliance that won the Lord's Day Act in
1907, and went on to form the Social Service Council of Canada.

There was Sara Libby Carson of the Young Women's Christian
Association, who, under Presbyterian auspices, and in association
with a handful of progressive women like Ethel Dodds, the head
worker of St Christopher House, Toronto, flung a network of social
settlements across the nation. Men like W.A. Riddell, later Ontario's
first deputy minister of labour, and Bryce Stewart, later of the
federal Department of Labour, worked under conviction in 1913 for
the Methodist and Presbyterian churches as they conducted the first
extensive social surveys of Canadian cities and rural areas. F.N.
Stapleford and J.S. Woodsworth, both Methodist ministers, had by
1916 become leading figures in the consolidation of social work
enterprises.

There was Beatrice Brigden, Quaker cum Methodist, who from
1913 to 1919 exhausted herself in weekly stands of social evangelism, lecturing on sex, marriage, and social problems in general, and
then joined A.E. Smith in his Peoples' Church in Brandon. And
church editors like J.A. Macdonnell of the *Westminster* and W.B.
Creighton of the *Christian Guardian*, who made their papers agents of
the Social Gospel. Agrarian leaders like Henry Wise Wood, R.C.
Henders, and E.C. Drury were not only influenced by the Social
Gospel but active proponents of it. Nor was the labour movement
without its contribution to the roster, with Unitarian A.W. Puttee
and Methodist James Simpson editing their papers, the *Voice* and
the *Industrial Banner,* from a social gospel standpoint.

To review the names is to rehearse the advance of the Social
Gospel in Canadian church and secular life over a generation. Nevertheless, many leading laymen in local congregations remained only
superficially influenced, and the postwar crisis brought out their
latent hostility. *The New Christianity* was written amid a protracted
effort by the most wealthy and prestigious members of Bland's new
congregation in Toronto to be rid of the disturber of their peace. He

survived, partly because of the strength of his own personality but also because a majority of his congregation stood behind him (a factor which was by no means decisive in such cases). Despite the contention which surrounded him, it was possible for Bland to write with hope, not only because the eye of faith could anticipate the ultimate victory but also because the Winnipeg and related strikes had not deflected the churches from the Social Gospel, the labour churches were still expanding, the church union cause was awakening once more, the tempo of farmer and labour political action was increasing, and the Liberal party had adopted an unprecedented social reform programme and entrusted its leadership to the chief Canadian exponent of joint industrial councils to bring peace to industry, William Lyon Mackenzie King. Progressive intellectuals were gathering their resources for the establishment of a journal, the *Canadian Forum*, and the Group of Seven had just given its first controversial show. All aimed at clarifying the Canadian consciousness, and challenging 'the hypnotic trance of a purely industrial and commercial ideal.'[34] In one way or another almost all these enterprises had been influenced by the Social Gospel. Bland had no illusions that an easy path lay ahead for the nation, however. 'A new, unquiet, distressful Canada is upon us,' he wrote;[35] but, equally, the signs had never been more promising.

The immediate constellation of reforms Bland was trying to nurture, however, rose to a peak of influence between the labour and Progressive victories of 1919-21 and church union in 1925, and did not return in force again for a decade. The Social Gospel movement sank into a trough of depression, eroded by a postwar recession which put a premium on funds, diverted by the backlash against prohibition and the cross-currents of church union, and compromised by the failure of the politics of righteousness and the unwillingness of the nation to embrace the economics of justice. Many were simply weary with well-doing. The intractability of social reality forced some into fundamental reconsideration of the mixture of social and religious ideas they had been promoting, while others sublimated their failures in a resurgence of the pacifist crusade. Radicals, who saw the face of power in social relations more clearly, could only hold their ground and await more propitious days. The revolution Lieutenant-Colonel Hamilton feared had not come.

In the meantime Bland had completed his ministry in the church
and begun a notable twenty-year career as a wide-ranging journalist
('The Observer') for the *Toronto Daily Star*. He threw what addi-
tional energy he had in the 1930s into stinging the councils of his
church into a more radical stance, flailing Toronto police for harrass-
ing reformers, addressing meetings for the new Co-operative Com-
monwealth Federation, encouraging the Fellowship for a Christian
Social Order, and working in united front organizations to counter
the spread of fascism and the clouds of war. Many could testify to
his ability still to rouse an audience even in his seventies. He died the
grand old man of the Social Gospel and reform in 1950.

It would be easy now to criticize *The New Christianity* on a
number of points. It reflects an age of platform enthusiasm with
which we are no longer comfortable. The history on which it is
based is too sweeping to be altogether plausible. Sociology and
anthropology have since badly dated the views of the time regarding
relations between race, religion, and society. Bland himself was too
much a Protestant for us to accept entirely his dissociation of
Protestantism from his anticipated new social order. On the other
hand, his treatment of Roman Catholicism shows no anticipation of
its later tendency to support fascist responses to the problems of
capitalism. He was over-sanguine in many of his characterizations of
the labour movement, though many who criticized him for it then
ignored his qualifications and also his introductory remarks that the
agencies of advance might at times be 'mistaken, sordid, violent,
even cruel.' In any case, to read the labour papers of that time is to
be impressed by the religious preconceptions behind their anti-
ecclesiasticism and their frequent use of Christian touchstones in
self-justification.[36] Superficially, the book's small proportion of ex-
plicit Canadian content together with a strain of continentalism
might make it seem a poor candidate for inclusion in a Canadian
social history series, but that would be an unfortunate commentary
on the parochialism of the Canadian mind. Bland's introduction
makes it clear that *The New Christianity* is aimed at Canadians first,
and the book was a product, among other things, of an intensely
Canadian mind.

As far as Bland's primary association of Protestantism and capitalism is concerned, Max Weber's famous argument that the spirit of
modern capitalism derived from the Protestant ethic has still to be

satisfactorily demonstrated. At least it can be seriously questioned,[37] and be proposed that socialism has similar claims to that paternity.[38] Nevertheless, Weber addressed himself to an association of first importance, and, by the same token, so did Bland. He was not wrong that Protestantism and capitalism were in the throes of profound change, but, in contrast to Weber, he believed too deeply in the force of the good in the movements of the time and appreciated too little the tenacity of the irrationalism of private capitalism.

The new social order has not ensued. The further development of labour, social welfare, and church has been won at the price of accommodation to a system of welfare state capitalism which has institutionalized poverty, deprived workers of any significant role in industry, and diverted the public with consumerism. It remains as true as in 1920 that an economic system which organizes other men for private ends necessarily fractures the community and perpetuates injustice.

Whether one touches the contemporary religious revolution at the point of the occult, the Jesus movement, theological debate, the experimentation in church forms, the oecumenical movement, to say nothing of the cross-fertilization of higher religions, it is evident that traditional Protestantism is at an end. Some might protest that Bland's Christian visions could not have survived in an emerging society of plural values, one which denied the state's allegiance to any single value-system. Undoubtedly the experience of the last half-century has given the lie to his vision of the righteous state in North America, but the canons of pluralism have problems of their own. Not the least of these is their short-circuiting of meaningful debate on the question of the nature of man in society, for pluralist dogma would preclude the application of any given answer to that question.[39] If *The New Christianity* does anything more than reflect the height of the Social Gospel and national hope in postwar Canada, it is to remind us that the fundamental question of ultimate social hopes remains. Can the vision of righteousness, the great prophetic hope of a time of peace and justice, be entertained any more as an historical hope at all, or is its function that of a transcendent reality which judges all our temporal constructions? The question is germane to the critique of Bland's book, and surely is also crucial to the scale of present action. Should we follow the intimations of pluralism that *The New Christianity* must be relegated to the ghetto of

Christian concerns at the end of the Age of Progress? Or should we
listen to Bland again when he says simply that 'the struggle will not
be over religious opinions, or political theories, though both are
involved. It will be over what touch men ordinarily much more
deeply, their livelihood and their profits ...'?

NOTES

1 United Church of Canada Archives (UCA), Toronto, Papers on Meth-
    odist Industrial Relations, 1920-2, C.F. Hamilton to T.A. Moore, 12
    June 1920. All other references below to Moore and Hamilton vis-
    à-vis *The New Christianity* derive from the small body of correspon-
    dence in this collection. For more on Hamilton, see Public Archives
    of Canada, Papers of Charles Frederick Hamilton; also Carl Berger,
    *The Sense of Power: Studies in the Ideas of Canadian Imperialism,
    1867-1914* (Toronto, 1969), pp. 248, 253. On Bland, see Richard
    Allen, 'Salem Bland and the Social Gospel in Canada,' MA thesis,
    University of Saskatchewan, 1961; and on the details of the context
    of *The New Christianity,* see Allen, *The Social Passion: Religion and
    Social Reform in Canada, 1914-28* (Toronto, 1971).
2 UCA, Salem Goldworth Bland Papers, 838, 'Comte,' Nov. 1897.
3 16 June 1920.
4 1 Sept. 1920.
5 *Toronto Daily Star*, 2 June 1920.
6 *Globe*, Toronto, 17 June 1920.
7 10 June 1920.
8 *Globe*, 17 June 1920.
9 *Toronto Daily Star*, 2 June 1920.
10 19 June 1920.
11 8 Sept. 1920.
12 19 June 1920.
13 10 June 1920. The Regina *Leader* simply reprinted the review in the
    Guardian.
14 11 June 1920. The Toronto *Labour Leader*, 4 June 1920, followed
    this approach, while the Hamilton *Labor News* like the *Western
    Labor News*, Winnipeg, reproduced the introduction to the book,
    which had the same effect.

15 See, for instance, the editors of the two early Canadian socialist
    papers, George Wrigley in *Citizen and Country,* 11 March 1899, pp.
    1, 3, and W.A. Cotton in *Cotton's Weekly,* as reported in J.C.
    Hopkins, ed., *Canadian Annual Review of Public Affairs, 1909*
    (Toronto, 1910), p. 306.
16 *B.C. Federationist,* 12 July 1918.
17 S.G. Bland, 'A Great Convention Hears Prophetic Words,' *Toronto
    Daily Star,* 10 Oct. 1942.
18 UCA, Henry Flesher Bland Papers, 'The Substance of an Address
    delivered in the Odd Fellows Hall, Addingham, Feb. 20, 1844, to the
    First Annual Festival of the Mechanics Institute,' which he had
    organized there.
19 See his *Universal Childhood Drawn to Christ* (Toronto, 1882), based
    on his sermon of 27 Nov. 1875 (Henry Flesher Bland Papers).
20 Bland Papers, 243a, 'Christian Perfection,' 4 Dec. 1880; 252b, 'The
    Twin Revelations of God,' 10 Dec. 1881; and 251c, 'The Ultimate
    Triumph of Christianity,' 22 Oct. 1881.
21 *Ibid.,* 245a, 'Significance of Conversion Cry,' 19 Feb. 1881; 258b,
    'Farewell Sermon on Cataraqui Circuit,' 17 June 1882.
22 *Ibid.,* 249c, 'Religion and Business,' 27 Aug. 1881; also 243c,
    'Joshua's Covenant,' 1 Jan. 1881; 244c, 'Isaiah's Vision,' 29 Jan.
    1881; 252c, 'Character,' 17 Dec. 1881.
23 *Ibid.,* 'My Intellectual Pilgrimage,' ms. of address, 16 May 1939.
24 See, for instance, the conference reports in the *Daily British Whig,*
    Kingston, 11 Feb. 1897, 16 Feb. 1899, 12 Feb. 1901; *Kingston
    Daily News,* 20 Feb. 1896, 11 Feb. 1897.
25 Bland Papers, 343, 'Man and the World Glorified in Christ,' 11 Sept. 1896.
26 *Ibid.,* 20, 'The New Christianity,' address to C.E. Union, Brockville,
    8 Nov. 1899.
27 See W.H. Magney, 'The Methodist Church and the National Gospel,'
    Bulletin, United Church Archives, Toronto, XX, 1968.
28 Methodist Church of Canada, *Journal of the General Conference,
    1894,* p. 300.
29 See J. Spelt, *The Urban Development in South Central Ontario*
    (Assen. Netherlands, 1955).
30 Bland Papers, 1, 'Human Nature,' 1885-6; 2, 'Men Needed,'
    1892; 381, 'Sermon to the Independent Order of Foresters,'
    16 June 1900; 419, 'The Canada of the Morrow,' 31 July
    1902.

31 Henry Flesher Bland Papers, Scrapbook 2, clippings 1888; 'Journal
    of the Montreal Methodist Conference,' 6 June 1896, pp. 26-7.
32 Bland Papers, 351, 'Discipleship Open to All Temperaments,' 28
    Aug. 1897; 909, 'A Study of Christian Churches and of the Church
    of the Future,' Dec. 1900; 910, Normal School lectures, 1900-1;
    386, 'Some Signs of the Times,' 23 Feb. 1901.
33 See references in Allen, *The Social Passion.*
34 F.B. Housser, *A Canadian Art Movement: The Story of the Group of
    Seven* (Toronto, 1926), p. 156.
35 'The Greatness of Times of Change,' *Grain Growers' Guide,* 23 July
    1919, p. 28.
36 Canadian labour papers merit a study like that of H.G. Gutman,
    'Protestantism and the American Labor Movement: The Christian
    Spirit in the Gilded Age,' *American Historical Review,* LXXII, 1
    (Oct. 1966).
37 There is an enormous literature on the subject, which has so far not
    resolved the issue definitively. For a recent critique, see Kurt
    Samuelsson, *Religion and Economic Action* (London, 1961).
38 Thelma McCormack, 'The Protestant Ethic and the Spirit of Social-
    ism,' *British Journal of Theology,* XX, 3 (Sept. 1969).
39 For an introduction to that issue, see the Epilogue in Donald B.
    Meyer, *The Protestant Search for Political Realism, 1919-1941* (Los
    Angeles and Berkeley, 1961).

The new Christianity

SALEM GOLDWORTH BLAND

Contents

To the Canadian soldiers,

spearhead of the

army of liberty in France,

spearhead of the

army of brotherhood in Canada

Preface

This little book is only a sketch. Some suggestions of the kind that is too exclusively regarded as practical, I hope, may be found in it. On the whole, its aim is, as from Mt. Nebo, to give a vision of the Promised Land. It does not attempt to minutely describe the roads leading thither. But then, probably, it is not given to any one as yet to map out very precisely the journey before us, for we 'have not passed this way heretofore.' It is my hope that these ideas which have gradually grown clear to me may help to increase the number of those who are willing fearlessly and resolutely to set out to find a way that may, after all, not prove so hard to find as it has sometimes seemed. The possible reproach of idealism is one to which Christianity itself lies too open to be feared.

I have tried to write impersonally. May I, then, here gratify myself by confessing how dear to me and how strong is the faith that my convictions and my hopes are shared by multitudes of my fellow-Canadians? I have lived in many parts of Canada. I have tried to understand the Canadian temper. Canada, I believe, has not yet found herself. The strain of the war has revealed her weaknesses — thoughtlessness, irresponsibility, divisive prejudice, worst of all, selfishness, sometimes in the extreme. But it has revealed, too, high devotion, quiet, unostentatious self-sacrifice, rare energy and resourcefulness.

There is in every nation a Jekyll and a Hyde, but not in every nation to-day is the struggle between the two so keen or the possibilities of its settlement so dramatic. The turn that our church life, our business life, our public life, may take in the next few years — which, indeed, I think, it is already taking — may be decisive and glorious. Canada has the faults of youth but also its energy, its courage, and its idealism. I believe it is possible that she may be the first to find the new social order and the new Christianity, and so become a pathfinder for the nations.

This preface would be incomplete if I did not express my great indebtedness to my friends, Professor W.G. Smith of the University of Toronto, who gave me valuable criticisms and suggestions, and Miss Ruth E. Spence, B.A., who kindly assisted me in reading the proofs.

SALEM GOLDWORTH BLAND
Toronto, March 1920

Introduction

The world-welter

THE WESTERN nations to-day are like storm-tossed sailors who, after a desperate voyage, have reached land only to find it heaving with earthquakes. In almost every country involved in the great struggle, the war without has been succeeded by a war within.

Of this turmoil, industrial or political as it may be, two things can be said. One is, that no Western people is likely to escape it, and certainly not the peoples of this Continent. The other is, that even in its most confused and explosive forms it is a divine movement. Mistaken, sordid, violent, even cruel forms it may assume. Strange agencies it may utilize. None the less no student of history, no one, at least, who has any faith in the divine government of the world, can doubt that these great sweeping movements owe their power and prevalence to the good in them, not to the evil that is always mingled, to us at least, so perplexingly and distressingly with the good.

If this be so, no clearer duty can press upon all who wish to fight for God and not against Him than to try to discern the good factors that are at work and the direction in which they are moving. This duty is the more urgent since no one can tell when the clamor and the dust may make it very hard to discern either.

In Canada, particularly, is this duty of careful analysis especially pressing. In no Western country, probably, has there been less experience of internal turmoil, less anticipation of it, or less preparedness against it. The attitude of Canada to life hitherto might almost be described as the attitude of a healthy, well-cared-for boy of fifteen, full of energy, full of ambition, with plenty of fight in him but still more good nature, whose only problems are the problems of the campus and of pocket money.

And yet it is conceivable that in no Western country may the turmoil of the next few years take a more acute form than in Canada. The youthfulness of the Dominion, the recency and frailty of the ties that bind the scattered provinces, the deep divisions of race and language and religion which criss-cross Canada in every direction, the high percentage of the new Canadians that have come, and recently, from the countries with which Canada has been at war, the large numbers of men who have now returned from overseas and who for different reasons, some of them unpreventable, are naturally and inevitably finding it difficult to discover their places in the tasks of peace — these conditions bring it about that Canada is not only not safeguarded, but is peculiarly full of inflammable material.

It is true that Canada in population is only one of the small nations, but it would seem as if none of the greater nations, since ramshackle Austria-Hungary fell to pieces, faces so severe an internal strain.

But, after all, nations never find their soul except through hard tasks. God educates peoples as He educates individuals, by putting them in tight places. This little book is written in the faith that the task of finding the right solution of Canadian national problems is so high and hard that only the deepest and truest soul of the Canadian people can achieve it, but, also, in the faith that Canadians, by the blessing of God, will be found equal to the task; and the chief purpose of what follows will be to show what are the good and beneficial elements in the turmoil, and how, with the least of strife and confusion, all who have other than selfish aims may co-operate in the divine movement.

There can be little fruitful constructive effort without hope, and, perhaps, we shall find, when we try to analyze the situation, that it has even more of hope in it than menace.

The aim of the following discussion is, as the title suggests, twofold:

First, to show that in the unrest and confusion of the civilized nations two principles, above all others, are at work; that these two principles are both of them right beyond question; and that the disturbance and alarm so widely felt are both due to the fact that these principles are finding their way into regions from which they have hitherto been largely excluded — to show, in short, that the whole commotion of the world, in the last analysis, is chiefly due to the overflow of the two great Christian principles of democracy and brotherhood.

Second, to point out the only kind of Christianity which is adequate to meet the situation, or in other words, to describe the Christianity which, we may hope, is taking form.

Part one

The New Social Order

Chapter 1

The overflow of democracy

THE HISTORY of the last nine hundred years in one, at least, of its most vital aspects is the history of the development of democracy. Perhaps in no other way can one so accurately discuss and estimate the progress achieved through this almost millennial period than in noting the successive conquests made by that great principle.

The first conquest was in the field of education. Modern democracy began with the rise of universities in the eleventh and twelfth centuries. Education had been the monopoly of the clergy, not, indeed, through any such design on the part of the clergy, but through the ignorance of the Northern races which had overrun Southern Europe and almost extinguished its culture, and through the unsettled and harassed condition of Europe which had delayed the growth of a new culture. It was only the clergy who felt that education was necessary.

It is one of the many inestimable services that the monasteries have rendered the modern world, that they preserved from destruction some of the precious flotsam and jetsam of that Greco-Roman literature which had for the most part been submerged, and that in these quiet retreats there grew up the schools which were to lay the foundations of yet nobler literatures.

Eventually, when a measure of peace came at last to the lands so long in distress and turmoil, the irrepressible impulses of the human soul for knowledge asserted themselves. The youth of Europe, eager to know, flocked in increasing numbers to the teachers who began to be famous, and the university took its rise.

Education placed in the hands of the people the key to other doors. As a natural consequence, democracy found its way into the jealously guarded realm of religion. After innumerable abortive, but glorious and not wasted, struggles for the right of the individual to find his own religion and dispense with ecclesiastical guides and directors, Northern Europe established the principle of democracy in religion in the great revolt known as the Protestant Reformation. That uprising was a very complex movement. Many motives mingled in it, but of these the desire for a purer faith was, probably, on the whole not so influential as the democratic passion for intellectual and religious freedom.

Concurrent with the overflow of democracy into the realm of religion was its overflow into politics. The evolution of political democracy is the distinctive glory of England. It is her contribution to world civilization as that of the Hebrew was monotheism, that of the Greek culture, and that of the Roman organization and law.

The barons, primarily in their own interest, wrested the Great Charter from a King who more recklessly and oppressively than his predecessors played the despot. In the provision of Magna Charta that the King should levy no more taxes without consent of the taxed was found the necessity of the coming together, first of the barons and the spiritual lords, later of the knights of the shire, and finally of the burghers of the towns — separate assemblies which soon coalesced and by their unification formed the English Parliament. English constitutional history from the reign of Henry III to the Revolution of 1688 is the history of the gradual supersession of the crown by Parliament, and of the ascendancy of the elective House of Commons over the hereditary House of Peers. The eighteenth century witnessed the development of Cabinet government; the nineteenth completed the great fabric of political democracy in those Franchise Acts which admitted to participation in the government —

In 1832, the propertied classes of the manufacturing towns;

In 1867, the artisan;

In 1884, the farm labourers;

In 1918, the women.

With these must be mentioned the Act of 1911 which constitutionally and decisively established the ascendancy of the popular House over the Peers.

England broke the trail which all other peoples that have accepted democracy have followed. The mobile and logical intelligence of France, slower through historical conditions to snap the feudal bonds, when it was at last aroused, at one bound outstripped England. Not content to limit, it swept away both monarchy and the House of Peers. A still more striking illustration of how the last may be first may yet be yielded by that great half-European, half-Asiatic people, so long, apparently, impenetrable to democracy, but now in the obscure throes of a revolution which despite its initial disorders and excesses, may, it is perhaps possible to hope, give to Russia the high honour of being the first nation to achieve the last conquest of democracy — its triumph in the economic realm. For it would seem impossible to doubt that that final triumph of democracy can be long delayed. Autocracy and aristocracy overthrown in politics cannot stand in economics.

He who will trace a river like the Mississippi from its source, and find it growing in hundreds of miles from a stream that may be waded to a great river a mile in width and a hundred feet in depth, does not need to actually follow the river to its mouth to be assured that it must reach the sea. Such a river cannot be diverted or dammed. Obstructions will only serve to make its current more violent.

This, then, would seem to be clear, that by an action as cosmic and irresistible as the movement of a great river, democracy is invading the industrial world. The time has passed for all temporary and makeshift expedients. A kindly spirit in the employer, improved hygienic conditions, rest rooms, better pay and shorter hours, will not secure equilibrium, though the spirit of good-will they tend to evoke may make further struggle less bitter. Profit-sharing furnishes no permanent resting place. It is merely a camping place on the journey. In the papers of February 12, 1919, appeared a significant despatch from London of the same date, describing the acute labor situation:

The labor situation reaches a crisis to-day in conferences between the government and three great unions, representing nearly 1,500,000 workers, the result of whose demands is awaited with keen interest by the entire labor world.

The unions are the Miners' Federation of Great Britain, membership 800,000; National Union of Railway-men, membership 400,000; and the National Transport Workers' Federation, membership 250,000. The unions are acting together, and it is believed they have agreed on joint action if dissatisfied with the result of the conferences.

The railwaymen's demands include a 48-hour week and control of railways by representatives of the managements and workers. This latter clause is considered a step toward nationalization, but an alternative has been prepared in the form of a commission of labor delegates and boards of directors.

William Adamson, leader of the Labor party in the House of Commons, speaking on the industrial situation, said that it was almost as menacing and dangerous as the war itself. He said that the principal Labor amendment to the reply to the address from the throne would relate to the causes of industrial unrest.

'I hope,' he continued, 'that no attempts will be made to disappoint the legitimate expectations of the working people. All sections of the people should understand that we have reached the stage when we have laid the cards upon the table and when the working classes will refuse longer to be treated as cogs in a machine or for mere profit-making purposes.'

In short, nothing will now satisfy the workers but a share in the control. The most hopeful scheme of harmony would seem to be some such arrangement as the Whitley scheme which has been officially endorsed by the British Government. The essential features of the Whitley scheme are the organization of all the workers in any industrial area, the organization of all the employers, the creation of joint committees representative of both groups to fix wages and determine conditions of labor. And this is not the end but the beginning. The end, at least of this phase of industrial evolution, would appear to promise to be the disappearance of the capitalistic control of industry. So far as industries are not owned and managed by the community, they will be owned and managed by the workers that carry them on. The revolution will be accomplished when the men of inventive and organizing and directive ability recognize that their place is with the workers and not with the owners. Capitalistic control must pass away. It has, no doubt, played a necessary and useful part in the social evolution. It has shown courage and enterprise. But it has been, on the whole, rapacious and heartless, and its sense of moral responsibility has been often rudimentary. When the managers on whom it depends desert to the side of the workers, it will be patent how little capacity or service is in capitalism, and how little it deserved the immense gain it wrung from exploited labor and skill.

The process may be harder and slower than even the most sober-minded would estimate, or it may be much easier and quicker; but the process has begun, and there can be but one end. Feudalistic industry must follow feudalistic land holding. Feudalistic landlordism went because the feudal lords were enormously overpaid in proportion to their services. When organizing and directive ability breaks the artificial bond that has associated it with capital, it will be seen how slight is the service capital has rendered and how enormously it has been overpaid.

Management is, of course, entitled to its wages, and under present conditions those wages must be relatively high, for managing ability is not abundant. What might be called the wages of capital have been unjustly high and are destined to fall until no man can afford to be a mere capitalist. To gain a livelihood he will be obliged to develop some productive function.

So long as industry must be maintained on a capitalistic basis, those furnishing the capital are entitled to a fair return on their investment, but the fashion of this capitalistic age passeth away. The control of money and credit is destined to gradually become a function of government.

A check must be placed on the fatal fashion money has of breeding money. Wages of labor, wages of invention, wages of superintendence, are just; profits of capital must grow less and less to the vanishing point.

The bitter conflict between capital and labor over the division of the profits will never be settled. It probably never can be settled. It will cease to be. Capital will cease to be a factor; only labor in the broadly inclusive sense of the term will remain.

The onward march of democracy, then, cannot be staid. It ought not. Democracy is nothing but the social expression of the fundamental Christian doctrine of the worth of the human soul. Democracies had found their way into human life before the revelation of the worth of the human soul in the redemptive work of Jesus Christ, but at their best, as in ancient Greece, they were restricted. Even that most glorious of all non-Christian democracies and, in some respects, most glorious as yet of all democracies non-Christian and Christian, the democracy of Athens, rested on a slave basis and excluded the man not possessing Athenian citizenship. But it was at least a noble anticipation, a sublime, if inconsistent, partial, and evanescent reaching-out after the democracy which Christianity can never be content till it has achieved, a democracy of religion, of culture, of politics, and of industry. The inherent dignity of every human soul must be recognized in every sphere of life. Heirs of God, joint-heirs with Christ – how is it possible to reconcile such august titles with servitude or subjection? A share in the control of church, community, industry is the Divine right of every normal man and woman.

Chapter 2

The overflow of brotherhood

THE CHURCH of Jesus Christ should not be alarmed at the inundating progress of democracy. She, of all institutions, should not oppose it. It is her child. But even democracy, with its majestic vindication of the worth and dignity of the humblest and least-endowed human soul, is not so distinctively and gloriously the offspring of Christianity as is the principle of brotherhood. The movement towards brotherhood, the great master-passion of our day, is just the overflow of Christianity from the conventionally religious into the economic realm. One might rest the divine claim of Christianity on this irrepressible impulse to overflow.

The ancient heathen faiths, with a few possible exceptions, did not seek to overflow. They asked only a strictly delimited area, definite times, definite places, definite gifts, definite ceremonial, observances and regulations. Outside that circumscribed area, life might go on as it would.

Even some forms of Christianity have shown little disposition to overflow. There has long been and still is a type of Christianity which fixes its eye on heaven and abandons earth. It is indifferent and acquiescent in regard to the affairs of this life, with no surge of passion for their purification and ennoblement.

This attitude has found expression in a hymn of John Wesley's which was once sung in its entirety but which, where it still lingers in our present collections, survives in a repeatedly and severely abridged form.

How happy is the pilgrim's lot!
How free from every anxious thought,
    From worldly hope and fear!
Confined to neither court nor cell,
His soul disdains on earth to dwell,
    He only sojourns here.

His happiness in part is mine,
Already saved from self-design,
    From every creature-love;
Blest with the scorn of finite good,
My soul is lightened of its load,
    And seeks the things above.

The things eternal I pursue,
A happiness beyond the view
   Of those that basely pant
For things by nature felt and seen;
Their honors, wealth and pleasures mean
   I neither have nor want.

I have no babes to hold me here,
But children more securely near
   For mine I humbly claim;
Better than daughters or than sons,
Temples divine, of living stones
   Inscribed with Jesus' name.

No foot of land do I possess,
No cottage in this wilderness,
   A poor, wayfaring man;
I lodge awhile in tents below,
Or gladly wander to and fro
   Till I my Canaan gain.

Nothing on earth I call my own:
A stranger to the world unknown,
   I all their goods despise;
I trample on their whole delight,
And seek a country out of sight,
   A country in the skies.

There is my house and portion fair,
My treasure and my heart are there,
   And my abiding home;
For me the elder brethren stay,
And angels beckon me away,
   And Jesus bids me come.

I come, — thy servant, Lord, replies —
I come to meet Thee in the skies,
   And claim my heavenly rest!
Now let the pilgrims' journey end,
Now, O my Saviour, Brother, Friend,
   Receivè me to thy breast.

As expressed in this hymn and still more in that spiritual classic, the *'De Contemptu Mundi'* of Bernard of Cluny, such a piety is not without its pathos and beauty and lofty idealism, but it is not Christianity.

It is only the pale bloodless spectre of Christianity. Christianity is a torrent. It is a fire. It is a passion for brotherhood, a raging hatred of everything which denies or forbids brotherhood. It was a brotherhood at the first. Twisted, bent, repressed for nearly twice a thousand years, it will be a brotherhood at the last.

Does Christianity mean Socialism? It means infinitely more than Socialism. It means Socialism plus a deeper, diviner brotherhood than even Socialism seeks. It abhors inequality. It always has abhorred inequality. It seems almost inexplicable that the censors in these days of panicky attempts at suppression of incendiary ideas have not put under the ban such words as these:

> My soul doth magnify the Lord,
> And my spirit hath rejoiced in God my Saviour.
>
> ...
>
> He hath showed strength with his arm:
> He hath scattered the proud in the imagination of their heart.
> He hath put down princes from their thrones, and hath exalted them of low degree.
> The hungry He hath filled with good things:
> And the rich He hath sent empty away.

LUKE 1:46-53

or these:

> Let the brother of low degree rejoice in that he is exalted;
> But the rich in that he is made low; because, as the flower of the grass he shall pass away.
> For the sun is no sooner risen with a burning heat but it withereth the grass, and the flower thereof falleth, and the grace of the fashion of it perisheth: so also shall the rich man fade away in his ways.

JAMES 1:9-11

'Nothing is hid,' was the word of Jesus, 'that shall not be made manifest, nor anything secret that shall not be known and come to light.' Many things have been hidden in that extraordinary amalgam that we call historical Christianity. St. Paul hid in it his peculiar idiosyncratic contempt of marriage and lack of reverence for women, and these elements worked out in the millennial denial of woman's rights and the abnormalities and tragedies of asceticism. St. Paul, again, and the unknown authors of the letter to the Hebrews and the fourth Gospel hid in primitive Christianity the Greek passion for metaphysics, and there emerged that perverse exaltation of dogma and orthodoxy which has, more than any other thing, withered the heart of the Church, smothered its fresh spontaneous life, kindled the infernal fires of heresy-trials and autos-da-fé. But Jesus hid something in historic Christianity, too, something deeper, diviner, mightier than any foreign ingredients added by other hands. Those commingling elements the Christianity of Jesus probably had to take up, test, and eventually reject. The only way, perhaps, in which the real meaning of Christianity could be discovered by men was in contrast with the innumerable and heterogeneous adulterations of it. We come to truth, it has been profoundly said, by the exhaustion of error. Humanity cannot apparently be sure of the right road till it knows all the wrong roads as well. So it would certainly have seemed to be with historic Christianity.

But deepest and most vital of all the elements that have found their way into historic Christianity is what Christ hid there – the equality of brotherhood. That hidden element, too, must find its way to the light. Early repressed, driven in, well nigh smothered, it has, nevertheless, never been extinguished, for it is the secret force, the most deeply vital essence of Christianity. As Bernard Shaw has said, it is not true that Christianity has been tried and found wanting; it has been found difficult and has never been tried. But in the profound words of Martineau, 'In the history of systems an inexorable logic rids them of their halfness and hesitancies and drives them straight to their appointed goal.' Not always by a straight road but by a sure one.

Nothing is more certain than that the human intellect must refuse eventually to acquiesce in that strange, illogical, and inconsistent jumble we call our Christian civilization. Something drives it irresistibly to consistency. The Christianity of Jesus means nothing if it does not mean brotherhood. Brotherhood means nothing if it does not mean a passion for equality. The story is told that when the Duke of Wellington, who, like so many other great soldiers of other times and of our own, was a devout man, was kneeling to receive the Communion in the village Church near his estate, a humble neighbour found himself, to his consternation, kneeling close beside the great Duke. He was rising at once to move away when the Duke put out his hand and detained him, saying, 'We are all equal here.' It was a fine spirit that the Duke showed for the time and in a country such as England was then. But it holds in it explosives of which probably the Duke did not dream. Equal at the table of their Common Lord! Then equal everywhere! Equality everywhere or equality nowhere! The soul of every man who has seen the divine beauty of equality must forever war against all limitations and impairments of it. Even human logic can not permanently tolerate such a fundamental incompatibility and irrationality as religious equality and social inequality sleeping in the same bed. Religious equality has already worked itself out in political equality. Even in aristocratic England the last vestige of political inequality has disappeared. The accepted formula is now – one man, one vote. It may be a harder problem to work out, but economic equality will be worked out to the same conclusion – one man, one share of all the conditions of human dignity and well being.

The keen satire of Charles Kingsley in *Alton Locke* will not always be justified:

'Faix, an' ain't we all brothers?' asked Kelly.

'Ay, and no,' said Sandy, with an expression which would have been a smile, but for its depths of bitter earnestness; 'brethren in Christ, my laddie.'

'An' ain't that all over the same?'

'Ask the preachers. Gin they meant brothers, they'd say brothers, be sure; but because they don't mean brothers at a', they say brethren – ye'll mind, brethren – to soun' antiquate, an' professional, an' perfunctory-like, for fear it should be ower real, an' practical, an' startling, an' a' that; and then jist limit it down wi' a 'in Christ,' for fear o' owre wide applications, and a' that. But

For a' that, and a' that,
It's comin' yet, for a' that,
When man an' man, the warld owre,
Shall brothers be, for a' that –
An' na brithren any mair at a'!'

Social inequality between human beings can never be a permanent relation. Ordinarily between normal human beings it is a hateful and demoralizing relation. It is twice cursed. It curses him who is down and him who is up.

It powerfully tends to make the one who is down and knows he is down, subservient, a truckler, a fawner. If a man is wise enough and strong enough to withstand the influence, the probability is that the very effort at resistance, unless he is very wise and very strong, will develop an unlovely and ungracious spirit of defiance, sometimes of hostility. In any case, human nature generally sours under it.

It is, perhaps, even worse in its effects on the one who is up. At the best he becomes condescending, affable, gracious, patronizing — intolerable attitudes every one. At the worst he becomes arrogant and insolent. Always he tends to become suspicious and cynical. He learns to distrust the forced respectfulness and obligingness everywhere shown to himself, and so comes to distrust courtesy and good-will in general.

H.G. Wells in his *The Future in America* inserts a picture of 'one of the most impressive of these very rich Americans.'

My friend beheld him, gross and heavy, seated in an easy chair in the centre of his private car, among men who stared and came and went. He clutched a long cigar with a great clumsy hand. He turned on you a queer, coarse, disconcerting bottle nose with a little hard, blue, wary, hostile eye that watched out from the roots of it. He said nothing. He attempted no civility, he looked pride and insults — you ceased to respect yourself ... 'It was Roman,' my friend said. 'There has been nothing like it since the days of that republic. No living king would dare to do it. And these other Americans! These people walked up to him and talked to him — they tried to flatter him and get him to listen to projects. Abjectly. And you knew, he *grunted*. He didn't talk back. It was beneath him. He just grunted at them!

Just as clear as the incompatibility of Christianity with social inequality is its incompatibility with business competition.

Competition for a livelihood, competition for bread and butter, is the denial of brotherhood. It is the antithesis of the Golden Rule. It is not the doing unto other men as we would that they should do to us. It is obedience to David Harum's parody of the Golden Rule, 'Do unto the other fellow as he wants to do to you, and do it fust.' The essential condition of competition is that always there shall be at least two men after the one contract, two men after the one job, two men after the custom, the patronage, the *clientèle* only sufficient for one. As a consequence, wherever competition exists, the success of one man always involves the failure of another. The man who gets the position knows that another man is suffering. The merchant who captures the trade knows that another must fail. The rule for success, as given by a highly successful business man of America, was, 'So conduct your business that your competitor will have to shut up shop.' The method is essentially disorderly and wasteful. Worse than that, it is inhuman.

It is difficult, indeed, to imagine how a more inhuman method of business could be devised short of methods which no man who had not ceased to be human would tolerate. Inhuman and dehumanizing. How deeply dehumanizing is seen in the effort of Christian men to justify it — the supreme illustration in our day of the morally blinding power of the accustomed, the familiar, and, above all, the profitable, which has made Christian men defenders of competition, of war, of the drink traffic, of the opium traffic, and of slavery.

Business competition to-day is, conceivably, as great an evil as ever intemperance was. Its working is more subtle, more widespread, more deeply destructive.

It hardens men. It dries up their natural and almost inextinguishable kindliness. It demoralizes them. It almost compels them to resort to crooked methods. It subjects them to temptations sometimes virtually irresistible. It presents them with the alternatives of failure and starvation for themselves and their loved ones or the doing of something, not right indeed, but which plenty of others do and which seems imperative. The honorable man has to compete with the dishonorable. The Hydrostatic Paradox of controversy, the Autocrat of the Breakfast Table has told us, lies in this, that as water in two connected tubes, however different their calibre, stands at the same level in both, so if a wise man and a fool engage in controversy, they tend to equality. The more demoralizing Hydrostatic Paradox of business competition is its deadly tendency to bring the honorable man down to the level of the dishonorable.

It is not always demoralizing. There are men strong enough to maintain their integrity, even sometimes at great risk. But the strain of it, the feverishness of it, the narrowing influences of it, still fewer men escape.

Under the shade and fallen needles of the pine forest, no other vegetation can grow. Under the absorption, the exhaustion, of the fierce business competition of America, little else than business shrewdness, business insight, business knowledge can grow. A thousand seeds of culture, art, music, philanthropy, religion, human fellowship, home happiness die permanently or fail to germinate at all in the American business man. The struggle, like a remorseless machine, seizes him as a young man and works its way with him till it flings him off at the other end of the process, a failure with a dreary old age of dependence and uncertainty, or a successful man broken in health at fifty, to spend the rest of his days in search of health, or with the leisure and the means to develop the old tastes but the tastes themselves atrophied by long and enforced neglect.

In the name of the brotherhood of Christianity, in the name of the richness and variety of the human soul, the Church must declare a truceless war upon this sterilizing and dehumanizing competition and upon the source of it, an economic order based on profit-seeking.

With profits not merely as an inducement but as the absolutely essential condition, the *sine qua non* not merely of success but of a livelihood, competition, even desperate competition, is inevitable. There is not usually the direct personal clash, the bloody or deadly combat, though these may be, but it is a life and death struggle none the less. In business competition, men are fighting with halters around their necks. They are fighting as wolves fight who know that the beaten one will be devoured by the pack.

How unfair and how futile under such conditions to heap reproaches upon the men who make what are called excessive profits! The risks are great. Should not a man make provision for them when he can? When, too, a man is immersed from boyhood in an atmosphere of profit-seeking, when in the talk around the meal-table and the conversation of his father with other men he gathers that profits are the measure of success, when in business he finds the whole energy and ingenuity and influence of men concentrated on profits, and men largely estimated by the amount of their profits, what capacity will be left after twenty years of such a life to distinguish between legitimate and excessive profits?

A profit-seeking system will always breed profiteers. It cannot be cleansed or sweetened or ennobled. There is only one way to Christianize it, and that is, to abolish it. That is, it may well be believed, the distinctive task of the age that is now beginning, as the abolition of the liquor-traffic was of the age that is closing, and the abolition of slavery of a still earlier age.

This whole present industrial and commercial world, ingenious, mighty, majestic, barbaric, disorderly, brutal, must be lifted from its basis of selfish, competitive profit-seeking and placed squarely on a basis of co-operative production for human needs.

How this tremendous transformation will be eventually accomplished, probably no one of this generation can foresee. All we can see is some initial steps.

A hint, it may be, is given in the well-recognized tendency of competing industries to escape competition by specialization. Thus they become co-operative. The same tendency to co-operative specialization is at work among professional men. Medical men specialize ever more narrowly. Lawyers elect to become authorities in a very narrow field.

Another principle of transformation may be found in the union of competing businesses under government regulation as to prices. Such combinations, while often disadvantageous to the public unless governmentally regulated, at least attest the increasing recoil from competition.

The main line of development, however, it seems altogether probable, will be the extension of public ownership, municipal, state or provincial, and national.

There is no diviner movement at work in the modern world. It is emancipating, educative, redemptive, regenerating. 'Whatever says *I* and *mine*,' says one of the wisest and most Christ-like of Medieval Mystics, 'is Anti-Christ.' The converse is equally true. 'Whatever says *we* and *ours* is Christian.' Public ownership, more extensively and powerfully than other human agency, teaches men to say *we* and *ours.* It teaches them to think socially.

To discredit and attack the principle of public ownership is to discredit and attack Christianity. It would seem to be the special sin against the Holy Ghost of our age. He who doubts the practicability of public ownership is really doubting human nature and Christianity and God.

What we are facing to-day is the issue between learning to do things together and a struggle between competing individuals, competing classes, and competing nations, so frantic and ferocious that in it our civilization may go down.

In these two chapters there has been the effort to set forth two at least of the dominating principles of the new social order. They are both embodied in a significant report adopted by the General Conference of the Methodist Church of Canada, October, 1918, in the city of Hamilton, Ontario. This report presented by a Committee on the Church in Relation to War and Patriotism was adopted, after a long and deeply earnest debate, in a reduced but still large Conference, with but four dissentient votes. It has awakened unusual interest as perhaps the boldest and most outspoken deliverance on the social question which any great Christian body up to that time had made.

REPORT NO. 3

II. Church leadership in the nation

Your Committee has had its attention directed to the work of the Church in the problems of reconstruction by some pregnant passages in the address of the General Superintendent, and by a Memorial from the Alberta Conference.

Even before the war it was widely foreseen that great social changes were imminent in the western world. This gigantic convulsion has precipitated the nations into the melting pot. Such an era summons the prophetic gifts of the Church, first, to the task of interpretation – to discern amid the turmoil and confusion the hand of God, and secondly, to the task of inspiration – to breathe into the hearts of men the faith, the courage, the patience, the brotherliness, by which alone the happy harbor can be won. And no Church is under a deeper obligation to assist in this two-fold task than our own. Methodism was born in a revolt against sin and social extravagancies and corruption. It was content with no aim lower than 'to spread scriptural holiness through the land.' Insisting on personal regeneration and all the implications therein, it transformed the face of England and saved that land from the excesses of a French revolution. To it the ideal of the Christian life was simply love made perfect. Without seeking at this time to commit the Church to a definite programme of economic policy, we would present for the consideration of our people the following statement which reflects our point of view:

1 The present economic system stands revealed as one of the roots of the war. The insane pride of Germany, her passion for world-domination found an occasion in the demand for colonies as markets and sources of raw materials — the imperative need of competing groups of industries carried on for profits.

2 The war has made more clearly manifest the moral perils inherent in the system of production for profits. Condemnation of special individuals seems often unjust and always futile. The system, rather than the individual, calls for change.

3 The war is the coronation of democracy. No profounder interpretation of the issue has been made than the great phrase of President Wilson's, that the Allies are fighting to 'make the world safe for democracy.' It is clearly impossible for the champions of democracy to set limits to its recognition. The last century democratized politics; the twentieth century has found that political democracy means little without economic democracy. The democratic control of industry is just and inevitable.

4 Under the shock and strain of this tremendous struggle, accepted commercial and industrial methods based on individualism and competition have gone down like mud walls in a flood. National organization, national control, extraordinary approximations to national equality, have been found essential to efficiency.

Despite the derangements and the sorrow of the war, the Motherland has raised large masses of her people from the edge of starvation to a higher plane of physical well-being and, in consequence, was never so healthy, never so brotherly, nor ever actuated by so high a purpose, or possessed by such exaltation of spirit as to-day — and the secret is that all are fighting or working, and all are sacrificing.

It is not conceivable that, when Germany ceases to be a menace, these dearly bought discoveries will be forgotten. Relapse would mean recurrence, the renewal of the agony.

The conclusion seems irresistible. The war is a sterner teacher than Jesus and uses far other methods, but it teaches the same lesson. The social development which it has so unexpectedly accelerated has the same goal as Christianity. That common goal is a nation of comrade workers, such as now at the trenches fights so gloriously — a nation of comrade fighters.

With the earthquake shocks of the war thundering so tremendous
a re-affirmation to the principles of Jesus, it would be the most in-
excusable dereliction of duty on the part of the Church not to
re-state her programme in modern terms and re-define her divinely-
appointed goal.

The triumph of democracy, the demand of the educated workers
for human conditions of life, the deep condemnation this war has
passed on the competitive struggle, the revelation of the superior
efficiency of national organization and co-operation, combine with
the unfulfilled, the often forgotten, but the undying ethics of Jesus,
to demand nothing less than a transference of the whole economic
life from a basis of competition and profits to one of co-operation
and service.

We recognize the magnificent effort of many great employers to
make their industrial organization a means of uplift and betterment
to all who participate, but the human spirit instinctively resents even
the most benevolent forms of government while self-government is
denied. The noblest humanitarian aims of employers, too, are often
thwarted by the very conditions under which their business must be
carried on.

That another system is practicable is shown by the recent statement of the British Prime Minister, that every industry save one in
Britain has been made to serve the national interest by the elimina-
tion of the incentive of private profit. That the present organization,
based on production and service for profits, can be superseded by a
system of production and service for human needs, is no longer a
dream.

We, therefore, look to our national government — and the factor
is a vital one — to enlist in the service of the nation those great
leaders and corporations which have shown magnificent capacity in
the organizing of life and resources for the profit of shareholders.
Surely the same capacity can find nobler and more deeply satisfying
activity in the service of the whole people rather than in the service
of any particular group.

The British Government Commission has outlined a policy which,
while accepting as a present fact the separation of capital and labor,
definitely denies the right of sole control to the former and, insisting
on the full organization of workers and employers, vests the
government of every industry in a joint board of employers and

workers, which board shall determine the working conditions of that industry.

This policy has been officially adopted by the British Government, and nothing less can be regarded as tolerable even now in Canada.

But we do not believe this separation of labor and capital can be permanent. Its transcendence, whether through co-operation or public ownership, seems to be the only constructive and radical reform.

This is the policy set forth by the great Labor organizations and must not be rejected because it presupposes, as Jesus did, that the normal human spirit will respond more readily to the call to service than to the lure of private gain.

The acceptance of this report, it cannot be too clearly recognized, commits this Church, as far as this representative body can commit it, to nothing less than a complete social reconstruction. When it shall be fully accomplished, and through what measures and processes, depend on the thinking and the good-will of men and, above all, on the guiding hand of God. But we think it is clear that nothing less than the goal we have outlined will satisfy the aroused moral consciousness of Canada or retain for the Churches any leadership in the testing period that is upon them. And in such an heroic task as this, our citizen armies will find it possible to preserve, under the conditions of peace, the high idealism with which they have fought for democracy in France.

Recognizing the greatness and complexity of the task before the Christian people of Canada, and the imperative necessity of united action by the Churches, we recommend that the suggestion of the memorial from the Alberta Conference be adopted, and that this General Conference invite the other Churches of Canada to a National Convention for the consideration of the problems of reconstruction.

Further, in order that our Church may give the most intelligent support to the movement, we recommend that our Ministers and people should acquaint themselves with such important documents as the Report of the United States Commission on Industrial Relations, the Inter-Allied Labor Party's Memorandum on War Aims, the British Labor Party's Programme of the new social order, and the British Governmental Commission Reports on Industrial Relations.

Your Committee outlines this programme in the profound conviction that it can be carried out only by men quickened and inspired by the spirit of Christ, and that for that Divine Spirit, working in the hearts of men, nothing that is good is too high or too hard.

Part two

The New Christianity

Chapter 3

A labor Christianity

A NEW social order is not more imperatively demanded than a new Christianity. Nothing less than this will suffice, nor will anything less be brought into being, in this crisis of transition. For while there are unchanging elements in Christianity, there are, it is equally certain, aspects that are constantly changing.

The devotion to the Lord Jesus Christ, which is the central and determinative principle of Christianity, is the least variable element; the institutions and dogmas by which that devotion is expressed and seeks to act upon the world, are the most variable.

Institutional Christianity is even more variable than dogmatic Christianity. It has varied greatly, is still changing, and its history shows that it is subject to the same influences as fashion the changing social order. This illuminating principle helps us to understand the past and to forecast the future of the Church.

During the last twelve hundred years or more, the Christian Church and the social order in Western lands have developed on parallel lines. Each has passed through two great phases and is now entering on a third.

I   THE ARISTOCRATIC OR FEUDALISTIC PHASE, A.D. 700-1500
The three centuries (roughly reckoning) from, let us say, A.D. 400 to A.D. 700 were, probably, the darkest in the history of civilization – darker even than the struggle of the last five years. They were the centuries of a struggle not so colossal in its apparatus of destruction, but seeming, even more than this struggle in its darkest hours, to threaten the extinction of civilization.

The Northern barbarians that had been pressing against the defences of the Roman Empire, as the yellow tides of the North Sea against the dykes of Holland, from the time of the inroads of the Cimbri and Teutons in the last decade of the second century before Christ, at last found entrance A.D. 378 when the Visigoths, who had been permitted to cross the Danube to find an asylum from the Huns, defeated the Roman armies and slew the Emperor in the great battle of Adrianople. From that year, with varying intervals of quiet, armies, or rather hordes, of men from the inexhaustible forests of Germany and Scandinavia, from the steppes of Russia and Central Asia, swept over lands for centuries accustomed to peace and weakened by bureaucratic despotism, inequitable and crippling systems of taxation, and, most debilitating of all, the essentially demoralizing influence of slavery. The mighty legions that had so long kept the frontiers inviolate vanished like a dream. The superb Roman roads and bridges fell into ruins. Fertile fields relapsed into wilderness. Towns decayed. Laws were forgotten. Cultivated languages with great literatures were replaced by barbarous jargons.

It was as when a country-side is devoured by a flood, and trees are uprooted, houses and barns dissolved or swept away.

Only one institution of the old Greco-Roman world withstood the waves, uprose above the yeasty flood in indestructible sovereignty — the Roman Catholic Church.

Out of the welter of overrunning barbarism — no law, no government, no protection except by superior force — the feudal system arose. The deep instinct for order and peace asserted itself. The strong man found a following. His tribe or clan, if he were a chieftain, his neighborhood, in any case, gave him service and maintenance, and he on his part gave the fullest measure of protection he was able to furnish. He became the feudal lord of a district. Through those stormy centuries that followed, when the savage people fought each other, and western Europe as it slowly struggled into order again was assailed by the Viking pirates on the North and West, by Hun-like Magyars on the East, and by the Saracens on the South, the feudal system was the only method by which over large areas any measure of security could be achieved. The strong man with his fighting force lived in his castle, and huddled under its walls lived the tillers of the soil, whom he at once in varying ratio protected and oppressed.

Some kind of relationship established itself among these feudal lords. One who by conquest or marriage had secured possession of specially large territories might out of these allot subordinate holdings to faithful followers, or by the same methods establish an overlordship over other lords. Eventually the deep and irrepressible instinct for unity and order lifted one of these families to the kingship of a group of feudal districts.

The feudal system was a varying system, the theory of which was never fully carried out, a system that had different origins in different countries and underwent different developments. The chief characteristic of it, as far as this reference to it is concerned, was its aristocratic character. Those men only counted who had enough land to support themselves and a body of fighting men. Whatever authority there was lay in their hands. The men who tilled the soil and practised the rude handicrafts of the age and carried on such beginnings of commerce as were possible, could find such imperfect security as there was only in accepting the despotic rule of one of these lords, knight or baron or count or duke as it might be, or more happily for them, in some respects, a bishop or monastery abbot. All sovereignty was in the mailed hands of these men or in those of the king, who in most of the countries slowly but surely established his control over his turbulent and recalcitrant feudatories.

It was the lowest form of order, the smallest degree of security, that feudalism provided. Legalized anarchy it has been happily called. But the measure of order and security it secured was probably all that was possible under such conditions, conditions under which an aristocratic system was the best system and, probably, the only and the inevitable one. Whatever judgment one may pass on the inadequacy and unserviceableness of aristocratic and monarchical forms of Government to-day, it ought never to be forgotten that we owe the beginnings of modern civilization to aristocracy, and its farther development to that outgrowth of aristocracy, monarchical government. Democracy in such a stage of civilization would have meant nothing but anarchy.

As under such semi-savage conditions no other kind of social organization could possibly arise than an aristocratic, so no other kind of ecclesiastical organization could meet the religious needs than an aristocratic. A democratically organized church could not have fulfilled the mission of the Church, could not, indeed, have existed. With great hordes of half-savage people precipitating themselves upon the Empire and almost extinguishing the ancient civilization, the only kind of Church that could grapple with the problem — the most formidable and appalling that civilization and Christianity ever had to face — was a Church organized on thoroughly aristocratic principles. Such a Church had been providentially prepared in the Roman Empire before its downfall. It has been already remarked that the one institution of the old shattered and submerged Greco-Roman civilization which survived the barbarian deluge was the Roman Catholic Church. We owe that Church, which has laid mankind to the end of time under unforgettable obligations, to the conditions which surrounded primitive Christianity and to the organizing, governing genius of the Latin mind.

Primitive Christianity, the devotion to the supreme Jew, Jesus Christ, we owe to the Hebrew mind. Transplanted among the Greeks, the simple, ethical, comparatively untheological and unorganized faith developed its latent philosophical implications. The Greeks gave it a creed. Transplanted simultaneously among the Latins, it was given an organization by that race whose superb and unexampled genius for government had made it mistress of all the countries around the Mediterranean.

The turmoil of erratic speculation within the infant churches with their motley converts gathered in from all kinds of religious and philosophic cults, and the ferocious persecutions from time to time launched at the helpless followers of the Christ, with their terrific temptations to apostasy or dangerous compromise, developed an aristocrat form of government. War and danger always call for the strong command. Christianity, threatened by erratic thinking and divisive controversy within and by deadliest attacks on the constancy of its people from without, found its salvation, as far as human agency was concerned, in the episcopacy, in large powers intrusted to the man who in the judgment of the individual Church was the wisest and ablest leader. The rule of the bishop was as natural and inevitable under such conditions as the rule of the captain on the ship at sea, the rule of the commanding officer in a fighting unit, the authority of the man recognized as leader in an unorganized group of farmers fighting a prairie fire. It is not wonderful that the bishops came to be regarded with veneration and their office as essential to the Christian Church. The episcopal office has earned the regard which it has enjoyed. The more fully one understands the historical conditions under which the belief in the indispensableness of episcopal organization grew up, the more reasonable one finds such a belief even if one is unable to admit its validity.

The same Roman genius for government which gave the principle of episcopacy its great place in the Church gave the Church also the papacy, and by a development as natural and, probably, as inevitable. The same necessity in troublous and dangerous times for large powers of command being held by the ablest man in the individual congregation or, later, in the group of Churches which came to be known as the diocese, developed the over-bishop, or archbishop, or metropolitan, or patriarch, as over-bishops were variously known, and over these again the supreme bishop, the bishop of bishops, the bishop of the great capital, Rome, who came at last to monopolize the title of Papa, or Pope, which originally had been given to every bishop.

The Papacy corresponds to the united command of the allied armies on the western front, which so swiftly and irresistibly transformed the war in that decisive area, and which will make illustrious till the Great War is forgotten the names of the great war-minister, Lloyd George, who so wisely and magnanimously brought it about, and the great general, Marshal Foch, who so magnificently justified it.

The Roman Catholic Church is the sublimest achievement of the organizing powers of mankind, and the unifying element in it, the capstone of that mighty structure, the key stone of the arch, is the Papacy. The Roman Catholic Church, or, as it might appropriately be designated, the Papal Church, is a greater construction than even the Roman Empire, of which it is the spiritual counterpart – vaster, more enduring, more firmly-knit, and infinitely more beneficent. The Pope corresponded to the Emperor; the bishops, to the provincial governors; the invincible legions which carried the Roman eagles into the swamps of Germany and the mountains of Caledonia, were surpassed in their daring and the tenacity of their conquests by their spiritual counterpart, the missionary monks.

It was this organization which had been providentially prepared for the anarchic and desolating period of the barbarian invasions, as Noah's ark for the Deluge, and not only as a shelter for the precious salvage of the submerged Greco-Roman civilization, but as a spiritual army which should conquer the conquerors, and on the debris of the greatest landslide of history fashion new gardens and habitations.

Latin Christianity, then, represents a distinctively aristocratic type of Christianity, the priest dominating the congregation and not controlled by them, the bishop dominating the priest, the Pope at the summit responsible to none but God. Such fashioning that great Church had received at the hands of men wise to give the Church such organization as the conditions demanded. It was this Church which the barbarian onset could neither shatter nor overpower. It was this Church which met the barbarians with a force and a sovereignty beyond their own. It asserted its moral and intellectual superiority. It overawed the men who, with the passions of men, had often the heart and still oftener the brain of the child. It put these turbulent warriors to school and struck to their hearts the fear of God and of the devil and of the Church.

No Church but an aristocratic one could have dominated such a situation. The very qualities which the modern man most resents in the Roman Catholic Church – its authority, its dogmatism, its spiritual powers of intimidation – were the qualities which enabled it to evangelize the vast heathen and barbarian masses. As in the state so in the Church, the centuries from the fall of the Roman Empire to the Protestant Reformation were centuries which called, though, it must be recognized, with lessening emphasis and with sporadic but multiplying exceptions, for the aristocratic principle. Feudalism and Roman Catholicism were the only possible systems.

II   THE BOURGEOIS OR PLUTOCRATIC OR
CAPITALISTIC PHASE, A.D. 1500-1914

Gradually, however, there arose in the aristocratically organized middle age a new power. This was the trading and manufacturing classes. As soon as the feudal nobility gave any measure of security, and much more extensively when kings grew strong enough to stretch the royal power over their turbulent feudatories, the irrepressible trading instinct asserted itself. English wool found its way to Flanders, French wine to England, the silks and spices and gems of the East to Europe. Busy and wealthy cities sprang up in districts favorable for manufacture and along the great trade routes between East and West. Kings, eager to assert their sovereignty over the anarchic barons, allied themselves with this new burgher class, which was on its part glad to support a power that promised it deliverance from such very imperfect and costly protectors as the feudal lords had shown themselves to be.

The Crusades, especially, stimulated trade and in the nearly two centuries (A.D. 1096-1270) during which the crusading spirit was active, the most notable feature of the social evolution of Europe was the rise of the towns.

The rise of the towns meant the liberation of the people. No buildings in Europe have more sacred associations than the old city halls of the medieval cities of the 'Low Countries, France, and Germany. They were the birth place of modern freedom.

Trade loves freedom and abhors all restrictions except such as are sometimes shortsightedly imposed by itself. The towns, wearied of the exactions of their castellated tyrants, won their freedom by purchase or by fighting, or co-operated with the king in reducing the barons to some measure of good behavior.

During the last five hundred years, and especially since the Industrial Revolution effected by the use of machinery, the merchant and manufacturing classes have been steadily climbing into power. They have superseded or absorbed the pre-existing aristocracy. The old families have died out or been transformed by a profitable and strengthening admixture of rich plebeians. The bulk of even such an imposing aristocracy as that of Britain is composed of creations of the last two or three generations, and these so largely from the ranks of wealthy brewers that there is truth as well as wit in the saying that the British peerage is the British beerage. The sale of titles at the price of large contributions to political funds is admitted and defended. Even in Great Britain, with its impressive array of ancient names, aristocracy has been largely converted into plutocracy.

In a constitutionally democratic nation like the United States there is no other aristocracy.

Now, if Church and State undergo a parallel development and re-act in the same way to conditions governing them both alike, what we might expect to find would be that, with the growing ascendancy in the social structure of the trading and manufacturing class (or to use a single term, though unfortunately one with a flavor of resentment about it, *bourgeoisie*), there would be a parallel ascendancy of the same class in the Church.

This is exactly what we do find. The aristocratic form of Christianity, which fitted into the feudalistic age, which was called for by the social conditions of that age, which was, indeed, probably, the only kind of Christianity that could have existed in that age, did not suit the freedom-loving, self-reliant, self-asserting, ambitious burghers. They resented the control which the clergy exercised over them, alike when it was well-meant and when it was selfish and tyrannical. Especially they resented the enormous sums which were extracted from them by the fees and taxes of priests, bishops, and the Papal Court at Rome. They resented, too, the Church's prohibition of interest. This condemnation, based on the Mosaic prohibition of interest, had not been found so unfair or vexatious prior to the sixteenth century when money was borrowed mainly for unproductive consumption, as for example, for war and for extravagance. Now when, in the great commercial development of that century, money was being borrowed for business with the prospect, almost the certainty, of profit, and interest became merely the sharing of profits, the Church's refusal of absolution to those guilty of taking interest was a serious factor in the growing hostility between the cities and the Church.

The Church, moreover, favoured sumptuary laws — the minute regulation of purchases and prices. As this well-meant legislation tended to restrict trade, it was disliked by the traders.

The immense capital locked up in vast ecclesiastical buildings and estates was naturally, also, the object of envy. Clerical immunities from municipal taxation, and episcopal jurisdiction over otherwise free towns added to the general irritation.

It might possibly have been foreseen that, sooner or later, a revolt would come and a new sort of Church would take form. That revolt came under Luther. Many motives conspired in it. With Luther himself and many of his followers the motive was a genuinely religious one. It was a revolt against the legalistic interpretation of Christianity and against the moral failure of the Roman Catholic Church. But with the mass of the city people, who were the main support of Luther, the motive was mainly a passion for freedom and only subordinately and sporadically a passion for a purer faith or a holier life.

In the new Church that was fashioned in varying forms in the northern races where the revolt was most general and thorough-going, one feature naturally predominated — the ascendancy of the *bourgeoisie*. That Church, or rather group of Churches which by seeming accident, but, perhaps, by that deeper philosophy which moves even through the seeming accidents of history, came to be known as the protesting or Prostestant Church, was the Church which suited a predominately middle class society as Roman Catholicism suited a feudal society.[1] Protestantism, in a word, is

1 'The "true inwardness" of the change of which the Protestant Reformation represented the ideological side, meant the transformation of society from a basis mainly corporative and co-operative to one individualistic in its essential character. The whole polity of the middle ages, industrial, social, political, ecclesiastical, was based on the principle of the group or the community — ranging in hierarchical order from the trade-guild to the town-corporation; from the town corporation through the feudal orders to the imperial throne itself; from the single monastery to the order as a whole; and from the order as a whole to the complete hierarchy of the Church as represented by the papal chair. The principle of this social organization was now breaking down. The modern and *bourgeois* conception of the autonomy of the individual in all spheres of life was beginning to affirm itself.'
Belfort Bax, *The Peasants' War*, p. 19.

bourgeois Christianity. It is the Christianity of the middle, or trading, classes. It was born where these classes were strongest – in Germany, Holland, Switzerland, England, France. It has exalted the middle classes and the middle classes have exalted it. It has been with them in their struggle and has shared their triumph. It sanctions their ethical standards, falls in with their tastes, emphasizes their virtues, is indulgent toward their faults, condemns their aversions.

It would almost seem that it was a consciousness of its specific class limitations which led the new movement promptly and decisively to turn away from the claims of the lowest class, though the distinct refusal of German Protestantism to champion the cause of the oppressed peasants in 1524 may be credited to the imperfect sympathies of Luther and his jealousy for the reputation of the new movement. Luther was a peasant's son, but his attitude to other peasants was one almost of contempt, mingled later with fear.[2]

Luther's glorification of the liberty of a Christian man, his stirring appeals to the German nobility to shake off the rapacious tyranny of Rome found response in other hearts than those he was addressing. His impassioned words, like hot coals kindling a fire wherever they fell, helped to bring to a head the discomfort which had been growing among the peasants. This was due, in part, to the increased cost of living, a fifty per cent advance, it has been estimated, from 1400 to 1415, for which the increased output of silver from the mines in the Tyrol and elsewhere was chiefly responsible. But the chief cause was the increased exactions of the German princes, sustained in their oppressive claims by the growing recognition of the Roman law, which found no place for the peasants except as slaves. Eventually, in 1524 the peasants drew up twelve demands which they submitted to Luther with an appeal for his support. Luther found the demands mainly just and urged the princes to make concessions, but strongly condemned any effort, in case the reforms were not granted, to secure them by violence. The demands were refused and the peasants rose. They were successful at the outset, as most of the professional

2 'The wise man saith: food, a burden, and a rod for the ass; to a peasant belongs oat straw. They hear not the word and are mad; then must they hear the rod and the gun and they get their due. Let us pray for them that they obey; otherwise there need be no pity for them. Let only the bullets whistle around them. Otherwise they are a hundred fold more evil.'
Letter to Rühel, De Wette, vol. II, p. 619.

soldiers of the princes were in Italy with the Emperor, Charles v, then at war with the Pope. On their return, these trained forces scattered the undisciplined bodies of peasants, already demoralized by wine and plunder and lack of leadership. The princes took a ferocious revenge. It is estimated that from one hundred to one hundred and fifty thousand peasants were slaughtered; many more were blinded and maimed.

Luther, angered and terrified by the uprising, had urged the princes on to the slaughter in words that are an ineffaceable blot on his memory:

First, they [the peasants] have sworn to their true and gracious [!] rulers to be submissive and obedient, in accord with God's command (Matt. 22:21), 'Render unto Cæsar the things that are Caesar's,' and (Rom. 13:1). 'Let every soul be subject to the higher powers.' But since they have deliberately and with outrage abandoned obedience, and in addition have opposed their lords, they have thereby forfeited body and soul, as perfidious, perjured, mendacious, disobedient rascals and villains are wont to do. [Later, Luther approved and justified the revolt of the Protestant princes against the Emperor to whom they had sworn obedience — so early had Protestantism one standard for the lowly and another for the high.]

It is right and lawful to slay at the first opportunity a rebellious person, known as such, already under God and the Emperor's ban. [Luther himself was certainly under the latter ban and, in the judgment of Roman Catholics, under the former.] For of a public rebel, every man is both judge and executioner.

Therefore, whosoever can should smite, strangle, and stab, secretly or publicly, and should remember that there is nothing more poisonous, pernicious, and devilish than a rebellious man [much more devilish in Luther's judgment than an oppressive prince!] Just as when one must slay a mad dog; fight him not and he will fight you, and a whole country with you.

If the civil government thinks proper to smite and punish those peasants without previous consideration of right or fairness, I do not condemn such action, though it is not in harmony with the Gospel, for it has good right to do this.

Therefore let him [a prince or lord] not sleep, nor shew mercy and compassion. Nay, this is the time of sword and wrath, not the time of mercy.

Such wonderful times are these that a prince can more easily win heaven by shedding blood than others with prayers.

He even makes the extraordinary statement, 'In 1525 the elector John of Saxony asked me whether he should grant the peasants their twelve articles. I told him, not one,' (Michelet, p. 448) — revealing a callousness which can only be characterized as brutal.[3]

Luther completed the severance of the new faith from the proletariat when he deliberately handed over his new Church to the control of the princes. In his complete distrust of the common people, it seemed to him that there was no other authority that could replace that of the bishops. So, despite the remonstrances of Melanchthon, a more oppressive tyranny was imposed on the Lutheran Church in Germany than had been exercised by the bishops, and the foundation was laid for that estrangement of the proletariat from the Church which has had such fatal results on both proletariat and Church in our time. On Luther rests the responsibility of converting the German Church into a branch of an autocratic government, as such distrusted and detested by the laborer in the country and the worker in the town, and of thus bringing about a condition of things which has earned for Protestant Prussia the reproach of being the least religious country of Europe.

Protestantism, then, by its very origin is Christianity shaped to suit the trading and manufacturing class. Now, what are the characteristics of members of this class? They are keenly but, in

3 'The Lutheran Reformation, from its inception in 1517 down to the Peasants'
   war of 1525, at once absorbed, and was absorbed by, all the revolutionary
   elements of the time. Up to the last-mentioned date it gathered revolutionary
   force year by year. But this was the turning-point. With the crushing of the
   Peasants' revolt and the decisively anti-popular attitude taken up by Luther,
   the religious movement associated with him ceased any longer to have a
   revolutionary character. It henceforth became definitely subservient to the
   new interests of the wealthy and privileged classes, and as such completely
   severed itself from the more extreme popular reforming sects.'
   Bax, *Peasants' War,* pp. 28, 29.

general, superficially intelligent, alert, watchful, ambitious, push-
ful, courageous, energetic, industrious, self-reliant, independent,
freedom-loving, intensely individualistic. They are honorable accord-
ing to the standards of their class, often generous when the business
struggle is not involved, but in the struggle itself they tend, almost of
necessity, to become hard and selfish. Their great aim has been to
'get on,' to make money, to rise to as high a social position as
possible, amid the vast opportunities of modern business to win and
retain great power.

Protestantism fits a people of such charactristics like a glove. It
exalts the rich man. It consults him and honors him, puts him forward
on every possible occasion, suitable or scarcely suitable. Knowing his
sensitiveness, it deals with him tactfully and deferentially.

It emphasizes the virtues conducive to business success – industry, thrift, sobriety, self-control, honesty, at least as far as the
law commands or as far as dishonesty would be plainly imprudent.

It disapproves the sins that hinder success or impair respect-
ability – such as indolence, profanity, intemperance, licentiousness,
and all overt transgressions of the law.

What would be the sensations of an audience to which a million-
aire manufacturer or broker or promoter was unfolding the secret of
his success, if he were to say, 'I owe my success and any distinction I
have been able to achieve to my honest effort to carry out the
Sermon on the Mount!'

For good and for evil, at the outset doubtless more for good than
for evil, now more for evil than for good, Protestantism is intensely
individualistic.

Christianity has its individualistic aspect. Protestantism has emphasized this. Christianity has also its social aspect. Protestantism
has largely ignored this.

Above all, Protestantism has lacked humility and pity. Naturally
so. They are the two virtues least called for in the business struggle,
the two virtues, indeed, most liable to prove embarrassing.

Here is where, probably, Protestantism most sharply differs from
Primitive Christianity and from the Christianity which was in the
mind of Jesus.

Protestantism is a fighting faith. It trains men to be self-reliant
and hard. Fair play is its substitute for brotherliness, and it often
finds it difficult to get as high as that.

The divine note of love is faint. Protestantism has never caught the passion for brotherhood. So it is not strange that, where the reviving spirit of brotherhood, which is the divinest movement in modern life, is strongest, there is the least drawing to Protestantism.

It is in the proletariat to-day that the sense of brotherhood is keenest. It is the proletariat which is the increasing despair of the Protestant Churches. Perhaps it is not too bold a generalization that, on this Continent at least – it does not seem so widely true in England – the working man who is most interested in the Church is least interested in labor organizations. He is the ambitious, individualistic workingman who is bent on emerging from his class. He is least class-conscious. He hopes to become affiliated with the master class.

The workingman who is most class-conscious, whose heart is set on the betterment of his class, is usually very slightly affiliated with the Church, if at all, and that affiliation is due, generally, to the appeal the Church and Sunday School make to his wife and children. Very frequently his attitude to the Church is one, not of indifference, but of resentment and distrust. He feels, though perhaps subconsciously, that the prevailing temper of the Church is one of self-advancement. The leading men in the Church are mostly those who have been most successful in strenuous self-advancement. Any man whose heart has been stirred with the passion for the common good is liable to be disappointed in seeking in the Church for the encouragement and sympathy that he craves.

Neither the Protestant nor the Roman Catholic Churches can claim to have inspired the Labor movement. At best it can only be said that, when the movement had struggled through the early days of conflict and persecution, the Churches reached out hesitatingly and half-heartedly a hand of fellowship in a spirit, partly of genuine desire to make amends for past dereliction, partly of condescension, and partly of fear.

But during the severity of Labor's early struggle, Protestanism, except in isolated and unofficial representatives, gave no assistance, not even its blessing, to what was the most profoundly Christian movement of the nineteenth century.

When it did not frankly sympathize with the masters in their difficulties with their unreasonable and discontented employees, it maintained a cautious neutrality. The first step to right relations between the Churches and Labor would be a frank confession that they failed to give Labor their help when Labor deserved and needed it most.

But perhaps this sympathetic attitude to Labor was too much to expect of a form of Christianity which had such an origin and such associations as Protestantism. Like the form of Christianity which it largely displaced in the freedom-loving northern races of Europe and America, it has rendered great services. Like that again, it was, perhaps, the only sort of Christianity possible under the conditions under which it took its form. It has helped to train an energetic, daring, self-reliant, and relatively honorable people. It has been the Christianity of a *bourgeois* epoch, and with the passing of that epoch it, too, will pass away or undergo a profound metamorphosis. It is a very different sort of Christianity that will meet the religious needs of the new epoch that the world is entering.

III   THE LABOR PHASE, A.D. 1914 –

We have seen how the trading and manufacturing towns pushed their way up during the later period of the medieval age and eventually overthrew aristocracy in state and Church, substituting a social and political order and a Church dominated by the business class. Similarly, since the middle of the last century, a new force has been pushing up in the *bourgeois* regime, destined, it now seems clear, to effect a similar transformation. This is organized Labor.

The most significant feature in the social development of the last hundred years has been the patient, persistent, oft-defeated, yet insuppressible struggle of the proletariat of the western world for human rights. The dead weight of the bygone ages was upon it. When had the men and the women who did the rough and necessary work of the world, smoothed the highways, dug the drains, built the houses and the bridges, carried the burdens over the mountains and across the seas, tilled the fields and cared for the herds and the flocks – when had they been other than the despised, ill-paid, ill-housed servants of the classes who through their fighting-power or their money-power could command the services of the toilers? What right had they to overturn the ancient order, an order which history recognized and the Church was willing to consecrate? Against the established order, against religious sanctions, against the combined authority of wealth and rank, against the legislative and military powers of governments, the workers had to carry on their new, uncharted, and desperate struggle unaided and alone. The Universities from their academic heights looked down on it with calm scientific interest. If any feeling was stirred, it was oftener contempt than pity. Even the Church of Christ was, with a few illustrious exceptions, unfriendly or timidly neutral. Nevertheless, in spite of calamitous setbacks, the movement made way against the public opinion of the dominant classes, against hostile legislation, against anarchic injunctions, against police and soldiers, and to-day Labor is the mightiest organized force in the world.

It is enthroned despotically in Petrograd and Moscow above the shattered ruins of the most imposing monarchy of the modern world. It is the strongest element in that welter of confusion and uncertainty to which the most powerful and compactly organized nation of modern times has been reduced by its insane ambition, the indignation of mankind, and the justice of God.

Labor is the uncrowned king of Great Britain. Wisely led, there seems no reasonable aim it cannot realize.

In the United States in the Summer of 1916, in a straight issue between Labor and one of the most powerful capitalistic groups, the President and Congress of the United States wisely and justly capitulated to Labor.

The futility of trying to 'smash the Labor unions' or to arrest the progress of the Labor movement is now sufficiently clear. As well try to smash a forty mile wide Alaskan glacier or arrest its onward march to the sea. Old precedents have lost their authority, old calculations and presuppositions fail or mislead. It is a new age the world is entering. As the determining factor in the social structure of Europe from 800 A.D. to 1500 was feudalism, and from A.D. 1500 to 1900 capitalism, so from 1900 onwards to the dawn, it may be, of still vaster changes as yet undescried, the dominant factor will be organized Labor.

If Labor, then, is to be the dominating factor in the age just opening, it becomes a question of deepest interest to discover the principles of the Labor movement.

A full answer to this question would be lengthy and might have elements of uncertainty, but the essential outstanding principles of the Labor movement are neither doubtful nor difficult to determine. They are three:

1 Every man and every woman a worker

The Labor movement has no place except for workers. Its essential demand is that every man and woman shall, during the normal working years, make a just contribution to the welfare of the social organism. It is determined that there shall be no place in society for idlers or exploiters. It is the deadly enemy of parasitism in all its Protean forms.

2 The right of every worker to a living wage

This is nothing other than the assertion, in the only form that makes it more than iridescent froth, of the great Christian principle of the worth of the soul. It is a very modest and restricted assertion of that great principle, but it is a more substantial and significant assertion than has been made anywhere else. The Christian doctrine of the infinite worth of the human soul becomes claptrap where this principle is not admitted.

3 Union

The Labor movement is based on the solidarity of the workers. It abhors competition. It represents the triumph of the we-consciousness over the I-consciousness. It organizes in unions. There have been few things in history that had more of the morally sublime in them than the way in which the individual has been called upon by the Labor movement to risk, not his comfort merely or his advancement, but his livelihood, in defence of some one whom he would never know but with whom he was linked in the sacred cause of Labor.

And these principles of the Labor movement are at the same time the characteristics of the corresponding Christianity of the new age. For, as we found an aristocratic type of Christianity in the aristocratic medieval period, the social conditions demanding the aristocratic organization in Church and State and permitting no other, and as, in the age which succeeded the feudal, a freedom-loving, competitive, individualistic class imposed its character on the social and the ecclesiastical organization, so institutional Christianity will undergo a third transformation and, in a society dominated by Labor organizations, will become democratic and brotherly.

Protestantism must pass away. It is too rootedly individualistic, too sectarian, to be the prevailing religion of a collectivist age. It is passing away before our eyes. Everywhere it reveals the marks of decay or of transformation. It must change or die.

Not to Protestantism, not to Roman Catholicism, belongs the age now dawning, but to a new Christianity which will, indeed, have affinities with them both but still more deeply with the Christianity of Jesus.

This Christianity, indeed, is already here. Like its Master when He came, it is in the world and the world knows it not. It is still immature, undeveloped, unconscious even of its own nature and destiny. It will receive large and valuable contributions from both the great historic forms of Christianity, not improbably from the Eastern, or Greek Christianity, as well. But in promise and potency the coming Christianity is more fully and truly here in the Labor movement than in any of the great historic organizations. Perhaps a more accurate statement would be, that the Labor movement needs less radical change than the great Church organizations to become the fitting and efficient Christianity for the new age.

It needs, in the main, but two great changes.

1 It must broaden

It must open its doors, as the British and Canadian Labor Parties are now doing, to include all kinds of productive work, of hand or brain. It must make room for all who contribute to the feeding, clothing, housing, educating, delighting of the children of men. It must include the inventor, the research scientist, the manager, as well as the manual worker; the men who grow things or who distribute them as well as those who make them; the professional class, who, on their part, must cease to regard themselves as other than men and women of labor. Labor must become, in short, the category to which all belong who really earn their living and do not seek to 'make' more than they earn.

2 Labor must recognize the Christianness of its own principles

I do not say Labor must become Christian. It is profoundly and vitally Christian in its insistence on the right of the humblest man or woman to human conditions of life, in its corresponding denial of the right of any human being to live on the labor of others without rendering his own equivalent of service, in its devotion to the fundamental Christian principle of brotherhood.

The Draft Report on Reconstruction, for example, prepared near the close of 1917 for the Labor party of Britain, is not only the ablest and most comprehensive programme of social reconstruction so far drawn up, but in its aims and methods and spirit it is profoundly Christian, a thousand times more Christian than the ordinary ecclesiastical pronouncement, though the name of Christ does not occur in it. The need is not so much that Labor become Christian, as that it become clearly conscious that it is Christian and can realize itself and win its triumph only on Christian lines.

It is not strange, after all, that among working men should arise the Church which is to give the truest interpretation of Christianity. The Lord Jesus was Himself a working man and brought up in a working man's home; His chief friends and chosen apostles were mostly working men. How can He be fully understood except through a working man's consciousness? The high, the served, the rich, the mere scholars, as such, are not fitted to understand Christianity. Individuals of exceptional character and insight may escape the limitations of their environment and education, but in any large community interpretation the working man's consciousness would seem to be essential. And, on any large scale, Christianity has never found such an expression as the Labor movement promises to give it — so essentially and predominately democratic and brotherly.

Labor and Christianity, then, are bound up together. Together they stand or fall. They come into their kingdom together or not at all. It is the supreme mission of the prophetic spirit at this fateful hour to interpret Labor to itself, that it may not in this hour of consummation miss the path. To turn away from Christianity now would be for Labor to turn away from the throne. But it will not. Mankind is in the grasp of divine currents too strong to be resisted.

Chapter 4

An American Christianity

IT WILL HELP US, perhaps, to understand still more clearly the religious revolution which is going on to-day concurrently with the social revolution if we survey the evolution of Christianity from another standpoint – the racial. In the preceding chapter the effort has been to show that Christianity in its organization and even in its spirit has been profoundly affected by its social environment and has changed as that has changed. The most superficial study of the history of Christianity reveals, moreover, that Christianity has been, also, deeply affected by the characteristics of each race among which it has made its home.

A. JEWISH CHRISTIANITY

The earliest form of Christianity was that which sprang up in Jerusalem immediately after the Resurrection and the ingathering at Pentecost. It was the Christianity of the apostles and of the first disciples. Perhaps it might be called a Christianized Judaism rather than a Jewish Christianity, for it was the old Judaism unchanged except by the acceptance of Jesus of Nazareth as the fulfilment of the national hope. The apostles remained good Jews, even stricter than before in their discharge of the duties of the old faith, and commanding through their strictness the respect of the Jews, James the brother of Jesus, in particular, being held in high esteem for his devoutness.

The chief characteristic of Jewish Christianity, it might almost be said, was its lack of almost all the features which have since been counted essential to a Church.

The ancient Jew, as has often been noted, markedly resembled the modern Englishman in many things, notably in an indifference to theological or philosophical speculation and in a strong sense of the value of the ethical and practical. These earliest Jewish Christians, accordingly, did not seek to analyze and systematize their faith. They did not seek to draw out its philosophical implications. They were interested in the construction neither of a creed nor of a theological system. They were content to hold their faith in Jesus as a vital loyalty and a great hope. Jesus was to them the long desired Messiah who would redeem Israel and establish the Kingdom of God upon the earth. That glorious consummation would take place when He returned, as they confidently expected He would, in the immediate future. Meanwhile, the door into the Kingdom of God stood open to all Jews who would accept Jesus as the Christ, and to such Gentiles as were willing to receive circumcision and identify themselves with Israel.

Overshadowed with the imminence of the Parousia, this Jewish Church of the first years had no interest in a reflective interpretation of its faith or in the elaboration of its organization. The apostles preached; alms were distributed to those of the disciples who were in need. No programme was drawn up for the future; no propaganda among the Gentiles was even dreamed of. The whole attitude was one of almost passive expectancy that clung to the ancient capital, the holy city, where the long-expected Hope of Israel would shortly, descending from the heavens, establish His throne.

Jewish Christianity had only the rudiments of a creed, only the simplest organization, and the most unelaborated and democratic form of worship. It was a seed with the germinating impulse unawakened, a bark launched and rigged but that had no thought of venturing out of the harbour.

This simple, undeveloped, undogmatic, unorganized, and Judaistic character of primitive Jewish Christianity is strikingly displayed in the early chapters of the book of the Acts and in the Epistle of James, which on most, at any rate, of the different hypotheses as to date and authorship is, at least, a witness to early Jewish Christianity.[4]

B. GREEK CHRISTIANITY

But the expansive forces residing in this undeveloped Christianity could not long remain inactive.

An important element in the population of Jerusalem in the time of our Lord was the Hellenist. This name was applied to the Jews who for various reasons, mainly for trade, had made their home in the commercial cities of the Levant. Here they had learned to speak the prevailing language of the countries around the Eastern Mediterranean, Greek, and had been, to a varying extent, intellectually broadened and quickened by contact with the Greek world. Large numbers of them returned to Jerusalem for educational purposes or

---

4 A later form of Jewish Christianity, the obscure Ebionitism of the second century, does not fall within the limits of this sketch. It was, probably, not so much a development of Christianity as a perversion of it.

to gratify their devout feelings, but they were regarded by the Palestinean Jews with something approaching contempt for their willingness to live away from the sacred soil of Palestine.

It was in the Hellenist mind, thus stimulated and developed by the Greek spirit, that the first development of Christianity occurred. To the Hellenist Stephen, the first thinker, the first controversialist, and the first martyr of Christianity, belongs the honor of first discovering the universal principle of Christianity, and his interpretation of Christianity brought about his own death and kindled a persecution which scattered the Christians of Jerusalem up and down the Syrian coast of the Mediterranean.

To some of these fugitive Hellenist Christians, partakers of the thought of the martyred Stephen, belongs the not less lofty honor of being the first to overleap the jealously guarded barriers of Judaism and to open the door of Christianity to the Gentiles. 'They therefore that were scattered abroad upon the persecution that arose about Stephen travelled as far as Phœnicia and Cyprus and Antioch, speaking the word to none save only to Jews. But there were some of them, men of Cyprus and Cyrene [and therefore Hellenists] who, when they were come to Antioch, spake unto the Greeks also, preaching the Lord Jesus.' Acts 11:19-20.

It is to be noted that it was, probably, this influx of Greeks into the Church hitherto composed only of Jews which made necessary a new name applicable to the composite body, and so it came about that 'the disciples were called Christians first at Antioch.'

A Church, in part Jewish but, probably, in still larger part Gentile, thus sprang up in Antioch, which became the mother city of Gentile, or world-wide, Christianity. From this centre the greatest of all Hellenist Jews, Saul of Tarsus, fired by that very universalism which had at first aroused the hatred of his bitter Jewish patricularism, carried Christianity westward through Asia Minor, Greece, Italy and, possibly, even to Spain.

Thus transplanted from the deeply and exclusively religious and ethical Hebrew mind to the predominantly speculative mind of the Greek, Christianity began to undergo an immediate transformation. The Greek mind, probably never equalled for its curiosity, its acuteness, its subtlety, could never be content to ask, what? It must also ask, why, and how? To it we owe science, philosophy, all our ordered thinking. Christianity, as a mere affection felt for Jesus

Christ or purely as a code of conduct, could not satisfy the Greek mind. The Greek mind, at first contemptuous of it as a mere vulgar superstition, fascinated at length by its rational monotheism, its lofty ethics, and, above all by the charm of its central figure, flung itself with ardor on the task of adapting this naive and untutored but fascinating religion to its own tastes and habits of thought.

A place was found for the Jewish Messiah in the philosophical world of the Greeks as the Logos, or Reason, of God, a familiar philosophical conception. Plato and Zeno were made His fore-runners. The principles of His teaching were dissected out of the traditions of His ministry and organized into a coherent body of doctrine. The acutest minds of Greek Christianity disengaged the great problems which were involved in the worship paid to Christ and, after centuries of speculation and of strife (not always intellectual only), achieved those great solutions which, whether in every respect permanently satisfactory or not, must forever be recognized as among the sublimest constructions of the philosophic intellect — the creeds of Nicaea and Chalcedon.

For good and for ill the simple, almost creedless Christianity of the Sermon on the Mount and of the Epistle of James had become through Paul, the author of the Fourth Gospel, the still more mysterious author of the Epistle to the Hebrews, and countless Greek dialecticians and theologians, the elaborately and authoritatively dogmatic system which has, almost till to-day, treated unorthodox opinion as the deadliest of sins.

The undue emphasis on the intellectual element in Christianity, the tyrannical control of human thought we to-day must deplore, but he who repudiates Greek Christianity must also deny that Christianity had any mission to the Greek mind, and that men have any right to think out their religious beliefs and adjust them to the rest of their thinking.

C. LATIN CHRISTIANITY

Latin Christianity cannot altogether be classed as a later stage than Greek Christianity. It was to a large extent a concurrent development. As far as its theological features were concerned, it was little more than the uncritical acceptance of dogmas worked out by the Greeks. But, eventually, the distinctive gifts of the Latin race asserted themselves and those races which had built up the Roman

Empire, or as subjects of it had become embued with its spirit, applied their organizing genius to the Christian Church and moulded the Church of the West into a replica of the Empire, and in such closely-knit fashion that, when under its own inherent weaknesses and through the irruption of the northern barbarians, that mightiest of all organizations of antiquity collapsed, the Church that came eventually and fittingly to know itself as Roman took its place and proved itself an even mightier organization, subduing restless and fierce peoples on which Imperial Rome had never been able to impose her yoke.

The Latin mind, then, with its reverence for order and law, its genius for government, its detestation of lawless individualism, discerned the possibilities of the Christian Church as an organization, and out of the simple piety of Jesus and the reasoned theology of the Greeks fashioned the mightiest instrument of discipline and order the world has ever seen.

Here, again, there may be a protest. This Latinization, or imperialization, of Christianity may be indignantly termed a perversion rather than a development. This only need be said in reply, that it would be difficult for anyone who has studied, without prejudice, the period between the overthrow of the Western Empire and the Protestant Reformation to deny the providential character of Latin Christianity. No other form of Christianity has as yet rendered so great a service to the race. It is questionable whether any other form of Christianity, even if it had been in existence, could at that stage have rendered so great a service. It was precisely those features in the attitude of the Roman Catholic Church towards her people which are most uncongenial to the Protestant temper which were the disciplinary agencies needed by the lawless, seething Europe of the Dark Ages to qualify it for the personal liberty the vindication of which has been the faith and service of Protestantism.

D. TEUTONIC CHRISTIANITY

The Greek mind moulded Christianity into a reasoned and systematized theology; the Latin, into an organization closely knit and marvellously efficient for the end to which Latin Christianity was largely and, perhaps, inevitably content to aim, — external control. Now, at least, we can see how inevitable it was that a third development of Christianity should take place after it had been transplanted among the Teutonic peoples. That development was slower in taking place than either the Greek or Latin forms. Those northern races which, until their conversion to Christianity, had stood almost completely outside the circle of ancient civilization, coming under the spell of a powerful religion and a civilization, even in its decay, majestic, were brought so thoroughly under the yoke that for centuries they were content to be ruled by a spiritual imperialism enthroned at Rome.

But that authority never ceased to be regarded by the northern races as a foreign one. The Teutonic peoples whose home lay outside the limits of the old Roman Empire were never Latinized in spirit. When they attained intellectual maturity and sought the free development of their own nature, they shook off the authority of Rome and brought to light those free and individualistic and spiritual germs in Christianity which, hitherto, in the luxuriant and stately growth of Greco-Roman Catholicism had remained almost dormant.

The Protestant Reformation, as has been noted, was a complex movement. It involved many factors. But fundamentally it was the outcome of the determination, not always clearly conscious, of the Teutonic peoples to discover a Christianity which should be consonant with that passion for freedom and that high sense of personal dignity which from the beginning had characterized the men of the Teutonic stock.

It is an interesting illustration of this that the movement of reform, or, rather, of revolt, which swept like a prairie fire over all Teutonic Europe that had never been permanently subdued by the Empire, flickered and died as soon as it crossed what had been the boundary of the old Empire, and that that boundary is still the dividing line between those countries of Western Europe which are preponderatingly Protestant and those which are preponderatingly Roman Catholic. The Roman Church held only what the Roman Empire had won. Only where the old Teutonic love of liberty had been subdued by centuries of the masterful and, on the whole, beneficent rule of old Rome did it cease to feel the spiritual rule of the new Rome alien and irksome.

Another illustration of how essentially Teutonic is the spirit of Protestantism is in the slight influence Protestantism has had on the Celtic peoples islanded in the Teutonic populations. Celtic Brittany is the most fervidly Catholic part of France to-day. Celtic Ireland remains solidly and deeply Catholic. Celtic Scotland, despite over-whelming Protestant influences, is till largely Catholic. Celtic Wales has become wholly Protestant, but it has seized and developed the least prominent and least Protestant of all the elements embraced in Protestantism, – the emotional and the mystical.

The rule of Rome under the Emperors and under the Popes had been the rule of the machine – a superb machine, ingeniously con-trived for what were conceived as the best ends, and operated with indomitable pertinacity and boundless devotion, but still a machine; and Protestant, or Teutonic, Christianity, in the last analysis, was the overthrow of the machine. To the Teutonic race belongs the honor of being the first on a racial scale to establish a religion without ceremonial or a priesthood or any privileged class whatever. Hebrew prophetism with its magnificent protest against ritual, and its cul-mination in the democratic simplicity of Jesus, now for the first time found recognition on a national scale.

Teutonic Christianity is the exaltation of the individual. It was born of individualism and glorifies individualism. It affirms the right and duty of individual judgment, the supremacy of the individual conscience, the privilege of the individual access to God. It finds the authority and proof of the Christian religion in its consonance with, and its satisfaction of, the capacities and needs of the individual soul.

The distance between the spirit of Latin and that of Teutonic Christianity, and, also, it should be noted, the distance between the twelfth century and the sixteenth may be seen in the two appeals of Abelard and Luther. Peter Abelard, a great and pathetic and only a little less than a heroic figure, was a Protestant, and in the best sense of the term, a free thinker, three hundred years before the Renais-sance and four hundred years before Luther. Accused of heresy by the saintly but censorious and bigoted Bernard, and brought to trial before a tribunal carefully packed by his relentless and unscrupulous adversary, Abelard, despairing of a fair hearing, refused to defend himself and appealed to the Pope. Another monk charged with heresy four hundred years later, inferior to Abelard in clearness and energy of thought but of more heroic moral fibre, before the most august assemblage Europe could gather, closed his defence with the undying words, 'It is not safe for a man to do aught against his conscience. Here I stand. I can do no other. God help me, Amen.'

Abelard appeals to the Pope, Luther to his conscience. That is the supreme contrast between Latin and Teutonic Christianity.

E. AMERICAN CHRISTIANITY

Since the revolt of the Teutonic peoples, the most remarkable phenomenon of Christian history has been the growth of a branch of Teutonic Christianity under the novel political and social conditions of the new world.

This has been a transplantation of Christianity quite as significant as any of its transplantations in the past, and the new soil has produced just as unmistakably new a growth.

Doubtless none of the great phases of Christianity in the past knew themselves to be new. Neither Greek nor Latin Christianity was conscious of any departure from primitive Christianity. Indeed, to this day, in their conception of the history of the Church, they persist in impressing their own type on that primitive and undeveloped type.

Teutonic Christianity took centuries to come to clear consciousness of itself and of its irreconcilability with Latin Christianity. It is not wonderful, therefore, that hitherto, as far as I am aware, American Christianity has been, if at all, very dimly and imperfectly conscious of the difference between its spirit and that of the Teutonic Christianity of the old world.

American Christianity has not yet arrived. It is only on the way. It has not yet found itself. It is not yet conscious of its own individuality, not yet self-reliant, independent. It is a youth, but a youth rapidly approaching manhood. Perhaps the characteristics that are unfolding themselves can be most clearly brought out by an attempt to show wherein it resembles, and wherein it differs from, each of the four great phases of Christianity which have just been under consideration.

1 AMERICAN CHRISTIANITY COMPARED WITH JEWISH

Compared with Jewish Christianity, American Christianity resembles the latter in its simplicity of creed, its emphasis on the practical and ethical, and (to a distinct and growing degree) in its brotherliness and democratic equality.

But its creedal simplicity is not the same as that of the primitive Jewish Church. That Church was wise in the brevity and simplicity of its creed, but it did not know its own wisdom. American Christianity is wise and knows its wisdom. It will not, like the Jewish Church, allow itself to be seduced into interminable theological controversies and into the superstition of orthodoxy. Seventeen hundred years of bitter wrangling and bloody conflict and cruel persecutions have taught it something. It has a short and a simple creed, not because it knows so little, but because it knows so much.

It differs, again, in its extensive and manifold organization, in the variety and elaborateness of its forms of worship, and, most markedly of all, in its attitude toward the present life. Primitive Jewish Christianity had no interest in the present social order. Intoxicated with apocalyptic visions, it stood on tiptoe awaiting with outstretched arms the return of the Saviour and the overthrow of this whole order by supernatural power. Its primary interest was eschatological. Its deepest feeling was expressed by St. Paul when he relegated all social relations and arrangements to the region of unimportance. 'But this, I say, brethren, the time has been cut short, that henceforth both those that have wives may be as though they had none; and those that weep, as though they wept not; and those that rejoice, as though they rejoiced not; and those that buy, as though they possessed not; and those that use the world, as not using it to the full: for the fashion of this world is passing away.' Cor. 7:29-31.

In this respect American Christianity is at the opposite pole. It does not look for the end of the world. It has largely ceased to believe in such a future and, where it still professes the apocalyptic faith, for the most part, it allows that faith little or no influence in actual life. American Christianity believes in the progressive and aggressive amelioration of things. It believes in this life and its glorious possibilities. It is bent on attaining them as no other sort of Christianity ever was before. It is steeped in optimism. It believes that the leaven of Christianity possesses the power to leaven all the relations and institutions of civilization. It believes that the fulfilment of our Lord's prayer, that God's Kingdom may come and His will be done on earth as it is in heaven, rests with the Church. Its real and, to an ever-increasing extent, its conscious and avowed faith is expressed by Dr. Henry Burton in the fine hymn:

There's a light upon the mountains and the day is at the spring,
When our eyes shall see the beauty and the glory of the King:
Weary was our heart with waiting, and the nightwatch seemed so
    long,
But His triumph-day is breaking and we hail it with a song.

In the fading of the starlight we may see the coming morn;
And the lights of men are paling in the splendours of the dawn:
For the eastern skies are glowing as with light of hidden fire,
And the hearts of men are stirring with the throbs of deep desire.

He is breaking down the barriers, He is casting up the way;
He is calling for His angels to build up the gates of day:
But His angels here are human, not the shining hosts above;
For the drum-beats of His army are the heart-beats of our love.

2 AMERICAN CHRISTIANITY COMPARED WITH GREEK

Of all the great historic forms of Christianity, it is the Greek from
which American Christianity might seem, at first sight, farthest removed. The punctilious orthodoxy of the former, its bitter doctrinal
polemic are utterly abhorrent to American Christianity. American
Christianity is more and more indifferent to theological agreement,
more and more tolerant of wide doctrinal differences. And it has
little interest in the great historic creeds.

Yet it is not so far away from the Greek spirit after all. It is
inquisitive and speculative and as interested as the Gnostics in great
sweeping theories of the universe. America is of all Christendom,
past and present, the most tolerant country, yet it is, at the same
time, a hotbed of religious speculation, even of religious vagaries. But,
at last, there has been born a kind of Christianity which can think and
let think, which is interested in thinking, but does not believe that
opinions determine a man's character here or his destiny beyond.

It should not be overlooked in comparing Greek and American
Christianity that American Christianity in its most thoughtful form
would have felt a great sympathy with the bold and free and comprehensive thought of the great Alexandrians, Clement and Origen.
It is the later and narrower and bigoted Greek Christianity, which
fittingly chose for itself the designation, the Orthodox Church, that
I have been contrasting with American Christianity.

3 AMERICAN CHRISTIANITY COMPARED WITH LATIN

The comparison of American and Latin Christianity is much more complex.

No two kinds of Christianity could well be more sharply opposed than these two in regard to the exalted claims of the clergy in the Latin Church. American Christianity is deeply and intensely democratic. Sacerdotalism in any form it instinctively rejects. The very idea of priest is passing out of its thought. The preacher it can appreciate. The competent ecclesiastical manager has its respect. The religious leader and pastor it can thoroughly understand and cordially recognize where genuine. But that any class of men should occupy a mediating position between God and man or possess a monopoly of any spiritual gifts is foreign to the American consciousness. 'Kings and priests unto God and the Father.' Those who are taught from childhood that they are kings are quite as conscious that they are also priests. The essential democracy of primitive Christianity has never established itself in any land before. This is the gift – and a great one – of American democracy to the Church.

What has been said of sacerdotalism holds true, to a still greater degree, of that thin, shadowy form of sacerdotalism, clericalism. The way in which the garb and badges of clericalism are disappearing in America is symbolical of the disappearance of the idea.

Latin Christianity, as we have seen, on account of the conditions of its origin and early history intensely autocratic, has always given a very humble place to the laity. Obedience and money were all that was required of them. The High Church theory, indeed, of the Roman Catholic Church and of the so-called High Church section of the Church of England is not a High Church theory at all. It is a High Clerical theory. The Church has been virtually identified with the clergy. Against the over-weening claims of Boniface VIII, Philip of France protested that 'Holy Church, the spouse of Christ, is made up not of clergy only but of laymen.' But that is not the working theory of Latin Christianity. A quaint medieval preacher suppressed what he thought was an undue bumptiousness on the part of his people by a sermon from the text Job 1:14, 'The oxen were plowing and the asses feeding beside them,' which, he showed his too forward hearers, clearly indicated the functions of the clergy, who were typified by the oxen, while the duty of the laymen was set forth by the feeding asses.

Luther's flight to the monastery when he became alarmed about his salvation was partly prompted by a picture which made a profound impression on him as a boy and haunted him for years. It was 'an altar-piece in a Church, the picture of a ship in which was no layman, not even a King or a Prince; in it were the Pope with his Cardinals and Bishops, and the Holy Ghost hovered over them, directing their course, while priests and monks managed the oars and the sails, and thus they went sailing heavenwards. The laymen were swimming in the water beside the ship; some were drowning, others were holding on by ropes which the monks and priests cast out to them to aid them. No layman was in the ship and no priest was in the water,' (Cambridge Mod. Hist. II., 109-110).

American Christianity is bent on an ever larger place for the laity in the Church and an ever-growing activity. The Y.M.C.A. and Y.W.C.A., the Young People's Society of Christian Endeavor and the Epworth League, the Laymen's Missionary Movement, the Men and Religion Movement, all illustrate the increasingly practical and lay aspect of American Christianity.

The Papacy, too, is another feature of Latin Christianity peculiarly out of harmony with characteristic American thought. The remoteness of the United States from the cradle of that institution, the hostility with which Washington inspired the young republic in regard to entangling alliances with European nations, its intensely American and democratic consciousness, all conspire to make the idea of a foreign ruler uncongenial to the American mind. The national consciousness of the United States is as exacting as religion. Its first commandment is, Thou shalt have no other country and no other ruler than the United States.

The authority of the Pope in the United States is maintained by being carefully withheld from all danger of challenge. The American Catholic is not conscious of any restraint in the tie that binds him to Rome because the rope is always paid out as freely as his movements require.

Again, it would seem that the Roman Catholic exaltation of the contemplative life over the active can never be accepted by American Christianity. There are no Catholics to whom the monastic life makes so faint an appeal as the Catholics of the United States. Perhaps a stronger admixture of the spirit of Mary might be beneficial, but American Christianity is emphatically a child of Martha.

On the other hand, however, there is much in Latin Christianity that appeals strongly to the American. His extraordinary genius for organization, in which he probably surpasses even the modern German whose great organizing capabilities have less of individual initiative, and the ancient Roman with whom, again, it was the characteristic of a class rather than of a people, dispose him to appreciate the great organizing skill that has always been shown by the Roman Catholic Church.

Further, the catholicity of that Church, its wonderful power to assimilate and build up within itself all races and languages and classes, cannot but appeal to a people engaged in solving a parallel problem. Modern American Christianity, moreover, is more and more unsectarian, even anti-sectarian. It does not glory in division and isolation. There is in it a growing passion for unity, a growing yearning for a strong, commanding, national type of Christianity that is much more akin to the imperialism of the great Popes, like Gregory VII and Innocent III, than to the parochialism and sectarianism that have generally and naturally been associated with Protestantism. American Christianity is fast losing all interest in denominationalism. All this is bringing it nearer to the temper of Latin Christianity.

4 AMERICAN CHRISTIANITY COMPARED WITH TEUTONIC

It may seem absurd to try to compare Protestantism and American Christianity, since the American Christianity that is here being discussed is mainly the Protestantism of America. But it is not exclusively the Protestantism of America. The Roman Catholicism of the United States shows, though less markedly, the same traits. And within the Protestant Churches of America another kind of Christianity is growing up as the butterfly develops within the chrysalis. And, moreover, it is not wholly within the organized Protestantism of America that the new Christianity is developing. There is an unknown but vast amount of the new American Christianity outside the organized Churches of America. A part of this was once in the organized Churches but has lost interest in their spirit and aims. A part of it has never been attracted by the organized Churches. Another great – probably the greatest – element in the coming American Christianity is the Labor movement which, as it has been suggested, needs only to be broadened and more consciously spiritualized to be identical with the coming true and indigenous Church of America. It is, indeed, a grave question whether the coming American Christianity will gradually capture and transform the present Churches or whether, as in the Protestant Reformation, the new wine will have to be poured into new bottles, and a new Church arise distinct from, and even in conflict with, the present Churches.

One thing, at least, is clear.

Protestantism in its present form will not survive. The very name is inadequate. It is not self-explanatory. It can only be understood by reference to another and earlier Church. It is negative. It has no positive or vital content. It carries with it the unhappiness and partialness of division. It is essentially and incurably sectarian. The more extensive and comprehensive the body becomes, the less intelligible becomes the name. If Protestantism should become really catholic, that is, universal, the name would become a complete misnomer.

American Christianity, so far as it still calls itself Protestant, only continues to bear the name through unthinking habit. As soon as it reflects upon the name, it must disown it. American Christianity is too essentially catholic and comprehensive, too little concerned with the past, too impatient of the old outworn disputes, to be content with a name that must always convey a flavor of division and controversy.

Protestantism, sectarian in its nature as in its name, is inadequate to express the genius of American Christianity. The dominating principle of Protestantism has been individualism, and the dominant note of American Christianity is fraternity. America is the chosen home of fraternal societies. It is Rudyard Kipling, I think, who has said that of the famous revolutionary motto, Liberty, Equality, Fraternity, the Frenchman cares only for equality, the Englishman is resolute for liberty and despises both equality and fraternity, while the American who knows neither liberty nor equality will forgive a man for anything if only he is a good fellow. The American loves a 'good mixer.' A shrewd French observer nearly twenty years ago in 'La Réligion dans la Société aux Etats-Unis' caught the spirit of this nascent American Christianity.

He found it, first, a social religion, and, as such, concerning itself more with society than with individuals; secondly, a positive religion, in its interest in what is human rather than in what is supernatural. It stands chiefly, he thought, for the idea of morality. It encourages a strong recognition of the fact that good people, without professing the same faith, are governed by the same rules of conduct, and that, if dogma divides, morality unites. He said:

The Americans make fraternity, the actual form of which is social solidarity, the essence of Christianity. The moral unity for which they strive under the name of Christian unity is only the co-operation of all for the increased establishment of fraternity and solidarity. High above sects whose diversity seems a matter of indifference to them, they organize a religion which pervades society throughout its length and breadth, and tends towards being only a social spirit touched by the evangelical feeling.

...

This moral unity is indeed a religious unity and a Christian unity; this positivism is a Christian positivism. American humanism has received from Christianity all the traditional, sentimental, and poetical elements which distinguish a religion from a philosophy. American positivism is only a Christianity which has evolved ... The American religion may be called a Christian positivism or a positive Christianity. It has received from the past the traditional and the evangelical spirit. Traditional, it preserves the names and the forms of the Churches even when it changes their customs; it develops them from the interior. Evangelical, it keeps the figure of Jesus Christ before all, even when it does not recognize his divinity.

...

Therefore it is not Protestantism ... The title of Christianity is the only one broad enough to designate it; yet this must be taken in its evangelical sense ... The American religion is living and fruitful because it is national.

To discern a distinct American Christianity in 1902 showed much more insight than its recognition indicates to-day. American Christianity has developed greatly since then and is now developing still more rapidly under the forcing conditions of the war and the great reconstruction. The work of reconstruction will not have been carried very far before the incongruity of this new type of Christianity with the hard, individualistic, militant spirit of Teutonic Christianity will become apparent to all.

When American Christianity comes to full and clear self-consciousness, when it, so to speak, finds itself, it will be found to have a very simple and brief and intelligible creed. Not a shallow creed, however, but a deep and vital one. It will put, probably, no other question to candidates for membership than the Apostolic Church put, Dost thou believe in the Lord Jesus Christ?

Its emphasis will be where Jesus placed it, not on opinions, but on spirit, the spirit of brotherhood.

Democratic it will, therefore, be as well, for democracy is bound up with brotherhood.

Finally, with a little creed it will have a big programme. It will live to establish the Kingdom of God on the earth. Its helpful, healing, redeeming, Christ-like activities will be infinite in the Christian and in the heathen lands.

And as pre-eminently practical, clericalism will die out of it. Preachers, teachers, missionaries there will be, but the gulf that has divided these from the laity will be closed. Sacerdotalism, even in its most attenuated and vestigial forms, will disappear.

Throughout this chapter, it is, perhaps, hardly necessary to add, the word, American, is used in its proper continental sense. By American Christianity is meant the new and distinct type of Christianity which is developing in the protestant churches of the United States and Canada and also, though less markedly, in the Roman Catholic. Politically distinct as these countries are likely to remain, socially and religiously they cannot escape the influences of neighborhood.

In some respects, as has been noted, the United States, on account of its republican constitution, its political rupture with the old world, and its more strongly developed self-consciousness, has been more favorable than Canada to the growth of that new form of Christianity, yet signs are not wanting, especially in that western section in which the coming Canada seems to be most clearly discernible, that the younger and smaller and so, perhaps, the more mobile country may outstrip her older and greater neighbor in the formation, out of, at least, the Protestant denominations, of a national Christianity, simple, yet free and varied, practical, democratic, brotherly, in a word, truly catholic. Institutions which have outlived their usefulness usually retain an appearance of strength until the hour of collapse. Denominationalism in Canada is still a stately tree, but the heart is dust.

Chapter 5

The great Christianity

BUT American Christianity is not final Christianity, nor even the highest and richest form of Christianity in sight, unless it blossom into a yet richer and more varied loveliness than it at present gives promise of. Of all actual forms of Christianity it seems to have the fairest promise, but it will probably prove to be only a tributary, though a great one, of a still mightier river.

Is it possible for us at this stage to discern at least the outline of the Great Christianity that is to be?

Certainly, every great historic form of Christianity has been tried by history and found wanting. As much of primitive Jewish Christianity as refused to merge in the large Catholic Christianity of the Greco-Roman world dried up into an unfruitful, bigoted, and eccentric heresy and perished.

Greek Christianity emphasized doctrine and tore itself by doctrinal disputes into a shattered, helpless welter of vituperative sects, powerless to spread the Gospel, powerless to withstand the Mohammedan — the shame and tragedy of Christian history.

Latin Christianity emphasized the organization and became the enemy of freedom and progress which, with few exceptions, every Roman Catholic people has had to fight and dethrone to escape intellectual and moral decay and death.

Teutonic Christianity has emphasized freedom and the rights of the individual. Like Islam, it has been a fighting faith. And judgment has fallen on it in its loss of unity, its bitter and wasteful sectarian wrangles, and the ferocious strife between labor and capital, the outcome of which may be one of the great tragedies of history.

Protestantism[5] has taught her people to fight for the rights and now is helpless before the selfish conflict of her own children that have learned too well her spirit.

In the great industrial conflict now reaching its height, one may safely prophesy Protestantism will perish — or be transformed.

She has taught her children to think; she has taught them to cherish freedom; she has not taught them to love.

---

5 It is, perhaps, scarcely necessary to remark that Protestantism is here being compared, not with Roman Catholicism, but with ideal Christianity. Roman Catholicism, too, has been a fighting faith, and in the appalling century and a half of religious wars that set in with the Protestant Reformation it was the older faith that first resorted to force.

Since by far the most of any readers this little book may be fortunate enough to find will be Protestant, it may be fitting and useful to point out more specifically the defects of Protestantism than the defects of other forms of Christianity among whose adherents, probably, the writer can scarcely hope to find many readers.

The Protestant Reformation, so far as it was not a struggle for liberty, national and intellectual and religious, was a doctrinal reformation. There was not much more of the spirit of Jesus, His gentleness, meekness, love, on one side than on the other. Erasmus understood Christianity on the whole better than Luther. Sir Thomas More was more Christian than John Calvin.

The Protestant Reformation was in its successful forms marked by little sympathy with the poor and the oppressed. It declined to recognize any duties to the serf except that of giving him the Gospel. Luther washed his hands of the peasants and calmly abandoned them to the savage vengeance of the princes when they refused to be satisfied with the liberty of Gospel preaching.

Protestantism has been, except in a few despised sects, militant, dogmatic, self-reliant, in a word, masculine. The gentler feminine characteristics of Christianity it has very slightly recognized.

When we think of the genius of Protestantism, we think of a humble monk, in the majesty of a conscientious conviction defying the two most powerful rulers of Europe, the Pope and the Emperor; we think of the indomitable sea-beggars of Holland and the heroic defence of Leyden; of the white-plumed Henry of Navarre and the battles of the League; of the splendidly audacious execution of Charles I., of Jenny Geddes' stool, the solemn League and Covenant and the bloody field of Drumclog; of the soldiers of Gustavus Adolphus, the Lion of the North, singing Luther's great hymn, *Ein'feste Burg ist unser Gott,* as they moved on to the glorious but dear-bought victory of Lützen; we think of the massacre of Drogheda and the undying defence of Derry; and of that typical Protestant and superb fighter, the rugged, dour, and unconquerable Ulster man whose unrelenting opposition and deep-rooted passion for domination have been so great an obstacle to Irish peace and the unity of the English-speaking world. Protestantism has had a great and a beneficent and a heroic history, but it has reproduced only imperfectly the Christianity of Jesus.

Meekness and long-suffering were outstanding characteristics of Jesus and of His early followers; they have rarely been outstanding characteristics of Protestantism. Perhaps Protestantism has been of necessity a man of war from its youth. Yet primitive Christianity encountered fiercer persecution and did not take the sword. Protestantism did not suffer long before she grasped the sword. She has, on the whole, followed Christ's precepts of non-resistance never when she had a fighting chance.

Primitive Christianity by patience and love conquered and Christianized the Roman Empire in three hundred years. Protestantism in more than three hundred years has gained not a foot beyond the territory won in the first rush of evangelical enthusiasm, and has lost territories she at first held. It is the demonstration of the futility of a fighting Christianity. Nowhere has the interaction of the two religions been associated with more fighting than in Ireland, and nowhere has Protestantism as an evangelical missionary force been more of a failure.

Gentleness, patience, humility have not been the strong points of Protestantism. She has been proud, vigorous, masterful, impatient of control, and to her have been given the kingdoms of the world. But not to her has been given the Kingdom Jesus promised to the meek.

In short, in Protestantism there is much of Christianity but there is also much simply of the old Teutonic spirit. Protestantism is not pure or primitive or ultimate Christianity. It is Teutonic Christianity, no more fitted to prevail than Greek or Latin Christianity. It is the faith of the fighter, the wrestler, the individualist.

Perhaps no community calling itself Christian suggests so remotely the tender name Jesus gave His disciples, 'my sheep.' Who, looking on a prosperous Protestant congregation in town or country, with shrewdness, vigilance, self-reliance written on almost every face, would think of saying, 'Fear not, little flock'? Freedom is what Protestantism has demanded and fought for, freedom to think for herself and take her own course and fight her own battles, every kind of freedom but one, the only freedom that need not be fought for, that can never be fought for — freedom to love and to serve.

Protestantism in its original form is passing away; it has run its course; its day is nearing its close. Where it has not caught the vision of the new and the Great Christianity, its churches are being deserted, its preachers are being seized with stammering lips and despondent heart.[6] Its spirit cannot solve the problems of the new age. It must become meek and lowly in heart. It must learn to love. Rich man and poor man must stand in its churches as they stand in the sight of God. Like medieval Christianity, it calls for a new Reformation — not a new creed but a new heart, the heart of a little child, humble, self-distrustful, not quick to resent, or even to see a slight, eager to love, delighting to serve.

Luther cannot help us here with his callousness to the wrongs and miseries of the peasants, nor Knox with his harshness and his militancy, nor Calvin with his hatred of those whom he thought God's enemies, nor the Puritans nor the Covenanters with their bigotry and their blow for blow and curse for curse.

Another deep lack is in Protestantism. In Isaiah's vision of the seraphim above the throne of God, 'each one had six wings; with twain he covered his face, and with twain he covered his feet, and with twain he did fly.' Two wings for service and four for worship! A Roman Catholic, meeting a friend who had become a Protestant, asked him how he liked his new faith. 'I like it well,' answered the other, 'but one thing I miss, and that is the spirit of adoration.'

How strange to us in Roman Catholic pictures are the faces of the saints upturned in adoration to the Mother and the holy Child! Protestantism does not produce faces like those. Shrewd, intelligent, alert, at best reliable, frank, kindly, they often are; humble, not often; reverent, adoring, still more rarely. Yet Goethe has said, 'The highest thing in life is the thrill of awe.' And Carlyle, too, 'Thought without reverence is barren and poisonous.'

Protestantism tends to be shallow, with the thinness and hardness and tinniness of mere intellectualism. It needs to tap great fountains

6 These words are written with reverent recognition of the innumerable forms of ministry to the bodies and souls of men that are being carried on by devoted men and women in the Protestant Churches, but, also, with the full conviction that these are slight and partial compared with the outburst of devotion and service which will be aroused when the vision of the new Christianity seizes great masses of men and women as the passion for freedom seized Germany in the years 1517 to 1524 or France in 1789.

   Never were the young men and women of Protestant lands so ready for a great task, but that task must be broadly Christian and broadly human. It must be a spiritual task but of a spirituality interwoven inextricably with politics, business, and sport.

of tenderness, humility, adoration, to be deepened, mellowed, enriched. Of the two ultra types of worship — the bright church, comfortable with plush cushions and glittering with brass work, where the people sit with wide-open eyes and curiously watch the preacher while he prays, and where the preacher with conscious cleverness clears up all the mysteries of life and *coloratura* quartettes display their technique (an ultra type, confessedly, and not common, but actual), and the dim church with the drooping Christ on the cross and pictured saints gazing in adoration and the congregation on their knees before the divine Presence in the Sacrament, one may be a convinced Protestant and yet believe the latter form of worship the more fruitful of the two.

American Protestantism needs new inspiration. So far as the past can yield this, it would seem that it should look particularly to three great leaders and saints — St. Francis of Assisi, St. John of England (to use W.T. Stead's deserved designation of John Wesley), and General Booth.

Perhaps the most winsome and Christ-like figure that Roman Catholicism presents, the loveliest flower in her rich garden of sainthood, is the poverty-loving, utterly lowly and loving, care-free and joyous Francis of Assisi, and perhaps, too, it may be said that no Christian character better deserves the study of Protestants. St. Francis is not an ideal figure; he lacks the balance and sanity of Jesus. Yet, perhaps, of all who have passionately set themselves to reproduce the life of Jesus, St. Francis in his utter humility, his complete unworldliness, and his overflowing tenderness can best bring home to Protestantism its hardness and shrewdness, its worldly-wisdom and its self-complacency. What a far-distant world is the world of the man who renounced all possessions, went about to preach and serve in coarsest, meagrest garb, who despised money and loved poverty, whose sympathies went out to birds and fishes, to Brother Fire and Sister Water, who could captivate robbers and even, it was believed, wild creatures of the woods, and at whose coming the Umbrian cities rang their bells and poured out with branches and flags to greet the mean little man with the shabby grey gown and the rapt, pale, worn face.

Let it be granted Protestant countries are more wealthy than Roman Catholic, more progressive, more successful in trade and manufacture, St. Francis gives us a glimpse into the simplicity and

childlikeness, humility and romance, that may sometimes find a
Roman Catholic atmosphere more genial than a Protestant.

Associated with the Franciscan order of tonsured monks and
cloistered nuns, there grew up a great society of men and women
taking a middle path between the world and the cloister — plainer in
dress, abstaining from the dance and the theatre, eschewing all
quarrels, praying and fasting more regularly, practising a more
systematic beneficence than ordinary Christians. And it is note-
worthy that, in 1882 on the seven hundredth anniversary of the
birth of Francis, Pope Leo XIII in an encyclical declared that the
institution of these Franciscan Tertiaries was alone fitted to save
humanity from the social and political dangers which threatened it.

Wesley and Francis are not far removed. The Saint of Epworth
was almost as ardent a devotee of poverty as the Saint of Assisi. If he
did not absolutely strip himself, he gave away immensely more. He,
too, had a passion for the souls of men, all of St. Francis' pity for
the poor, and he won a wealth of reverence and love. He was a far
wiser man, living in a more rational age. But he was not only extra-
ordinarily competent. He knew, too, his own competence. There is a
wild flower grace of the childlike in St. Francis that we miss in the
far more intelligent and commanding figure of Wesley.

Primitive Methodism had much of the enthusiasm and devotion
and joyousness of the Franciscan brotherhood. Francis' friars and
Wesley's helpers had a common unworldliness, joyousness, and
passion for the souls of men. But even as the Franciscan movement
diverged from the ideals of St. Francis, so Methodism soon developed on lines of its own. It has preserved much of the evangelical
fervor and the practical helpfulness of its original inspiration. Considered in its direct and indirect effects, its union of evangelicalism,
mysticism, and practical kindliness, there has been no other Christian movement which has combined such a measure of purity with
such vastness of influence. In genuine Christian influence it has surpassed even the Reformation. Modern Christianity (and there is a
distinguishable modern Christianity) is of all forms that Christianity
has assumed the nearest to the Christianity of Jesus, and in its
fashioning the Methodist Revival has been the chief agency. Yet
Methodism has not realized the ideals of its human founder. It did
not perpetuate his unworldliness. It failed, as R.W. Dale pointed out,
to the great loss of Christendom, to develop the ethical implications

of his great doctrine of perfect love. It cherished his memory and his organization, but it refused to inherit his dread and hatred of riches. Its very thrift and industry and morality have been its undoing. It became, in great measure, like Protestantism in general, a *bourgeois* religion, eminently suited for people who want to get on in the world. Its chief abhorrence has never been of social inequality and injustice but of the wasteful frivolities and vices, dancing, card-playing, theatre-going, and, pre-eminently, intemperance. The Report already cited shows, however, a new spirit at work in the Methodism of Canada, a spirit in which Wesley would rejoice, and it is not in Canadian Methodism only that it is at work.

A still closer resemblance obtains between the Franciscan order and the Salvation Army than between the former and Methodism. No two movements, perhaps, so widely apart in time and methods are so closely akin. Poverty, humility, obedience, love are the dominant features of them both.

Francis is a more winsome figure than General Booth but incomparably less intelligent and efficient. Francis awakened a great religious revival but probably wrought little improvement on the face of Europe — on its ferocity, chronic warfare, sensuality, oppression of the poor. The Salvation Army has redeemed countless victims of poverty and vice. It has probably proved itself the most effective agency in all history for the salvation of the down and out.

The Order and the Army have the same limitations.

1 Both are too exclusively inward and individualistic. They do not deal adequately with conditions and causes, the Franciscan movement not at all, the Salvation Army very timidly. The weakest element in the latter is its willingness to accept gifts from even those who have made their wealth out of the degradation of men and women, and its seeming reluctance to engage in any drastic social reforms which might dry up such bounty. It is content with ambulance work, and even the most devoted and heroic ambulance work will never stop the war.

2 Both, too, are sectional; fitted only for the few, the enthusiasts. Each has cared for the saint; neither has made provision for the ordinary man. Christian perfection, in the thought of Francis and of General Booth, is for the man who withdraws from the ordinary

work of the world, turns away from its culture, crucifies a thousand human instincts, breaks all the strings of the human lute but one. Both movements organized by these great saints are eccentric, abnormal. Neither is workable on a catholic, or universal, scale. Both sectionalize the holy life.

What is needed to-day is another leader, a leader for the ordinary man. The ordinary man is neither saint nor fanatic, neither preacher nor monk; he would be bored to death if he had to sing or pray or meditate all day; his joy is in building bridges and planning railways and ripping up the matted prairie sod with gasoline engines; he likes his wife and children and does not feel called upon to become a missionary to China or Central Africa. The need is for the leader who can show this ordinary man how to bring the truest love and the deepest piety into the ordinary, commonplace, work-a-day life, revealing the glory of God, not alone as gilding the cold snows of Alpine peaks or bathing the distant desert with unearthly beauty, but transfiguring the city street, the cozy home, the quiet fields where lovers walk at even.

Francis, Wesley, Booth — the time has come for each section of the Christian Church to remember that 'all things are hers: whether Paul or Apollos or Cephas.' We Protestants may think the Roman Catholic Church less likely to appropriate our saints than we theirs. This judgment of ours may be right or wrong, but we have no right to pass it until we ourselves have recognized the limitations of Protestantism and set ourselves heartily to appropriate the great elements of the Christian life that are the distinctive glories of Latin Christianity. Protestantism, too, has its own peculiar glories. Neither great division of Christendom is adequate to meet the religious needs of to-day. The hour has struck for the great Christianity.

The future belongs neither to Roman Catholicism nor to Protestantism. Roman Catholicism is too aristocratic and distrustful of freedom. The modern man will no more go back to medieval Christianity than to medieval feudalism. There is a drift from Protestantism to-day, but the drift from Roman Catholicism has been far greater. To fulfil its destiny, Roman Catholicism must accept freedom of thought; magnificently democratic as it has been from the beginning in some respects — the chair of St. Peter being accessible to the humblest peasant's son — it must accept a deeper and wider democracy.

Protestantism, on the other hand, must become heart-broken over its divisions, religious and social. It must become more brotherly, more lowly, more worshipful, in a word, more childlike.

It is unthinkable that either of these great forms of Christianity will pass away. They will change. They are already changing, and each, as it changes, moves toward the other.

Thought and life move through conflict to unity. Thesis – antithesis – synthesis – that is the great law. The great and, perhaps, inevitable stage of antithesis that has divided Christendom for four centuries is drawing to a close. Latin Christianity needed Protestantism. It was the Protestant Reformation that inspired the counter-reformation. Roman Catholicism owes to Luther and Calvin a purer faith and a new lease of life. Today the noblest and more energetic types of Roman Catholicism are found in Protestant lands, and the service of Protestantism to Roman Catholicism is not yet finished.

Just as certainly, Protestantism needs Roman Catholicism. Some exposition of this has already been attempted. It is hard to see how any one who believes Roman Catholicism to be a tissue of errors can account for its extraordinary tenacity of life. Why should God preserve it unless because its mission is not yet accomplished?

Far apart and deeply antagonistic these two great forms of Christianity may seem, but, after all, it is an inescapable law on this earth that two people who try to get as far away from each other as possible must meet at last; and hatred is nearer love than is indifference. Human nature wearies of antagonism, and the longer it lasts the warmer the welcome for its passing.

Like denominationalism, this four hundred year old antagonism seems a mighty tree but, like denominationalism, it is hollow within. Some day the great winds of God will arise, and when they begin to blow, this tree, too, will fall.

The thirteenth century was one of the great centuries of Christian history. In it feudalism reached its height, and chivalry its fullest flower. In it Gothic architecture and medieval philosophy reared their noblest monuments. It was the century of the greatest of medieval, or, perhaps, of distinctively Christian, poets, Dante, the greatest of Christian theologians, Aquinas, the greatest of Popes, Innocent III, the two most winsome of saints, St. Francis and St. Louis of France. In all its greatness, the thirteenth century is distinctively Roman Catholic. The nineteenth century, also, is another of the less than half a dozen of the greatest of Christian centuries, and it is distinctively a Protestant century. Its great achievements in geographical and astronomical discovery, scientific investigation, increase of human comfort and wealth, and above all its unparalleled extension of liberty – bear all of them the Protestant stamp.

These two centuries have thus established beyond dispute the right of those two great historic forms of Christianity to the lasting reverence and gratitude of mankind.

Roman Catholicism has cherished the divine principle of unity. At great cost it has preserved unity. It has not been equally careful of the divine principle of liberty.

Protestantism has gloriously fought and suffered and died for liberty. It has never highly valued unity. It has even gloried in division. But unity is a diviner thing than even liberty. Liberty is precious only as the indispensable condition and pre-requisite of true unity.

It is a lovely and thrilling hope that the twentieth century may prove to be the century of the Great Christianity, the Christianity which will extinguish neither Latin nor Teutonic Christianity but comprehend and blend them, the simple, yet free and varied, democratic, passionate Christianity of all who love the Lord Jesus Christ and seek His Kingdom on the earth, the Christianity which was the first and will be the last.

This, at least, can be said, that the unparalleled problems of social and political reconstruction facing the world to-day can be rightly solved only by a great religious devotion, and it is difficult to see how that devotion can be secured except by a unification of the great Churches of Christendom and their common baptism into the spirit of primitive Christianity.

And let no one say the Great Christianity is only a beautiful dream.

Already, in that forever holy strip of land where towns were reduced to heaps of dust and trees to splintered trunks, where earth was gashed and torn as men never gashed and tore the kindly bosom of mother earth before, and where beautiful human bodies were mutilated and destroyed with a fury unknown in history, there the Great Christianity has disclosed itself. There at the mouth of hell unfolded the sweetest flowers that ever bloomed on earth. There in the brotherhood of the trenches became visible the Great Christianity. There Anglicans, Baptists, Congregationalists, Methodists, Presbyterians, Salvationists, and every other kind of Protestants, aye, and Roman Catholics, kneeled together to commemorate the suffering and love of their Common Redeemer, the Soldier-King.

'Father,' wrote a Manitoba boy to his father from the trenches, in the spring of 1917, 'we have a religion here but, father, it is not the same as yours. You don't like the Catholics or the Church of England, but, father, we love everybody here. We are all one. And, father,' the boy went on, 'when we come back, our religion is going to blow yours sky-high.'

A prophecy not as yet fulfilled but not, perhaps, beyond fulfillment. Certain it is that our soldier boys will never crowd into our churches as they crowded to the colors till those churches are the home of a Christianity that has the breadth and the brotherliness and something, at least, of the heroism of the Christianity of the trenches.

But something more must be said about the Great Christianity.

It may be that Latin Christianity and Teutonic combined do not represent the full splendor and power of Christianity, and that the drastic social changes which must be carried out in the next quarter of a century, or even in a briefer period, call for the re-inforcement of another race and another sort of Christianity.

The distinctive Greek Christianity of the first five or six centuries made its contribution and passed away with the vanishing of the original and pure Hellenic race. But there is a Greek Christianity which has found a new lease of life and a new home in that race which has largely replaced the Greek in his own home and has diffused itself over most of eastern Europe, the Slavonic. There is a great Christianity which is still called Greek, but which is rather Slavonic Christianity, and which might more narrowly and specifically be called Russian Christianity, after that people who constitute the largest section of Greek Christianity and promise to be the most influential.

It may well be that the Great Christianity which the world so desperately needs will be neither Latin nor Teutonic Christianity nor both in combination, but a blend of Latin and Teutonic and American and Russian Christianity, and it does not seem unlikely that the contribution of the last of the four may be the most precious and vital of them all. Perhaps in the part Russia is destined to play in the next fifty years will be found the most striking example in all history of how it is God's way to choose the foolish things of the world that He may put to shame them that are wise; and the weak things of the world that He may put to shame the things that are strong; and the base things of the world and the things that are despised that He may bring to nought the things that are.

The Slav has been the Cinderella of the European sisterhood. Perhaps we might say, the ugly duckling. From a military point of view he has been no match for the Teuton. In the long struggle of the last thousand years between the Teuton and the Slav, the Teuton has nearly always showed himself the stronger. For centuries he has ruled over the Slav. In the industrial arts, in all that pertains to the utilization of natural resources for the material well-being of men, in agriculture and mining and manufacturing and trading, the Slav has been immeasurably more backward. Mastered and oppressed by the Teuton on the West, subjugated for centuries by the Tartar on the East, the Slav has remained until yesterday a people forgotten and despised, shrouded in poverty, ignorance, mystery. And now out of that twilight he has stepped, ignorant, fanatical, and in his ignorance or superstition capable of ferocity, yet essentially the most childlike, the most religious, the most brotherly, the most idealistic of European peoples. What other people call their country, what the Russian calls his — *holy* Russia?

The peoples of the West, especially the Teutonic or the Anglo-Saxon, are weak where they are strong. It is their practicalness that has given them their high place; it is their practicalness which keeps them from the highest. It is hard for them to believe in a Holy City. If they do believe in it, they do not care to seek it till they are sure of a practicable road. But the Slav instinctively believes in a Holy City, and only needs to be told where it is to be found to set out forthwith over rivers, bogs, and rugged mountain ranges.

And it is just these things the Western world needs in this crisis — the spirit of the little child, the spirit of brotherhood, the sense of the pre-eminence of religion, the idealism that will risk everything for a dream.

The first movements of the awakened Russian may be unsteady. His new found freedom may act on him with intoxicating, almost deranging power. But they know little of the real Russian soul who dread the liberation of that long-prisoned soul and its free play on the Western world.

In the material ground-work of our civilization, its farming, its mining, its building of steamships, of railroads, of modern cities, the Teutonic races have taken the lead. They have builded the house. Now, it may be, when the finer problems arise of living in the home in harmony and helpfulness and in a high and holy spirit, it is the Salv who, in his turn, will take the lead. The Greek, the Italian, the Frank, the Spaniard, the Anglo-Saxon have successively held the premier place. The day of the Slav may now be dawning.

Nor yet is our forecast of the Great Christianity complete. It may be that there awaits us, though in a more distant future, a still more striking illustration of how God chooses for honor the despised things of the world. Of all races the most despised, the most op-pressed, has been the African, and that not for generations or centuries but for millenniums. Europe, Asia, and America have all made Africa their servant. The dark Continent stands pre-eminent in suffering and in service. But it is in suffering and in service that He, too, the Coming King, has been pre-eminent. One reason why Africa has been the hunting ground of the slaver from immemorial times is because in the African nature immemorially and inextinguishably is the readiness to serve. All other races love to rule; some of them, like the Latin and the Teutonic, have been intensely proud, greedy of power, and averse from service. The African race is the one race which has by nature the spirit of Him who came not to be minister-ed unto but to minister. The African race, too, is of all races the most childlike, the most care-free, the one most ready to delight in simple things and the things of to-day. The white race, in compari-son, are old, vigilant, suspicious, anxious, care-worn. There is no question which, in these respects, is nearest the ideal of Jesus. The greedy, ambitious spirit of the Western nations, never contented, their delight in to-day always poisoned by the fear or the fascination of to-morrow, is far from the spirit of Jesus. It may be that the white man will yet have to sit at the feet of the black, and that, when Christ is glorified, it will be that race that has, beyond all other races, trodden Christ's path of suffering and service which, beyond all others, will be glorified with Him.

The re-action of the uncounted millions of Asia on Chris-tianity — the contributions of the ancient and deeply experienced brown and yellow races to that religion in which alone they can find their fullest development — is another fascinating subject for enquiry and speculation; but these influences, potent and inescapable as they promise to be, fall outside the limits of the period considered by this book.

Conclusion

THE TASK before Western civilization today, it is probable, is the greatest civilization has ever faced. It is a complete reconstruction that is demanded. It must be accomplished with speed. All the Western nations are involved. There have been other reconstructions as drastic, but either they have been permitted a much longer period of development, or they have been confined to much smaller areas.

The struggle will not be over religious opinions, or political theories, though both are involved. It will be over what touch men ordinarily much more deeply, their livelihood and their profits, and the war has seemed to show that men will sacrifice their lives more readily than their profits. It will be a struggle no class can escape.

The readjustments would be difficult enough in themselves if men engaged in them in the calmest and kindliest spirit. But many who will be foremost in the task of reconstruction bring to the problems the bitterness and distrust engendered by centuries of cruel wrong.

Nothing but Christianity can carry the Western peoples through this unparallelled crisis. But it must be Christianity in its purity and its fulness, not a Christianity wasting its energy on doctrinal controversy, broken by denominational divisions, or absorbed in taking care of its machinery. It must, in short, be a Christianity neither intellectualized nor sectarianized nor institutionalized.

It must be a Christianity, born as at the first in the hearts of the common people, simple, democratic, brotherly; like a tree, its top in the sky but its roots deep in common earth; treating institutions, even the most venerable, as the mere temporary contrivances that they are; with the faith of Jesus in the human heart and in the ultimate triumph of love, and a willingness, like His, to find a throne in a cross.